# FEAR
# UNMASKED

# FEAR UNMASKED

## DISCOVERING THE TRUTH OF THE CORONAVIRUS SHUTDOWN

### CLAY CLARK

Fedd Books
P.O. Box 341973
Austin, TX 78734

www.thefeddagency.com

Published in association with The Fedd Agency, Inc., a literary agency.

ISBN: 978-1-949784-45-9
eISBN: 978-1-949784-46-6

Printed in the United States of America

First Edition 15 14 13 12 11 / 10 9 8 7 6 5 4 3 2

# TABLE OF CONTENTS

# INTRODUCTION

*"Education is the key to unlock the golden door*
*to freedom."*
– George Washington Carver

Close your eyes and picture for a moment a place and time where America has completely stopped. Our once bustling streets are now empty. The Starbucks drive-through no longer has the standard ten-minute line wrapped around it, and Chick-fil-A is no longer packed Monday through Saturday. Picture a weird parallel universe where the streets of Los Angeles have no traffic and the only drama being reported about the NCAA's March Madness is that it was cancelled. Visualize walking through the nearly always, twenty-four-hour energetic and urgent Times Square without running into a single person (other than the occasional police officer who has been assigned to go out patrolling to make sure that you are not violating ever-changing protocol).

Unless you have been living under a rock, you cannot help but to see and hear the fear-inducing coronavirus updates relentlessly reigning down upon you. It's confusing, unprecedented (you've probably heard that word a hundred times in the last week), and it seems like no one really knows what's going on. Yesterday you heard that 2.2 million beloved Americans are predicted to die from the contagious coronavirus, but today you heard that less than 200,000 Americans are predicted to die. Should you be worried or should you be relieved? Things change every day and it seems that no one knows what is going on.

As I drove to the gas station yesterday to fill up my wife's suburban with unleaded gas that is now at the coronavirus-caused-low-low-price of $1.56 per gallon, I could sense panic and fear everywhere. The man filling up his large Ford F-350 with gasoline was wearing a mask, and the streets were eerily empty. In fact, the people who were actually desperate enough to go out and buy the food and goods they needed were going in and out of the gas station while practicing "social distancing," so it was awkward to watch them walk past each other while trying to avoid one another while still being kind. Since mid-March of 2020, our federal and local governments have been pushing us, pleading with us, and mandating us to help stop the spread of the virus with the same intensity and focus that I used to employ as a kid to avoid physical contact with the cute girls in the first grade because of the "cooties" virus that I knew all girls had.

Even as I briefly isolated myself from humanity to write this book, I cannot escape the fear-inducing messages being pitched at me from every direction. Even now, when I sit down in my "Man-Cave" to write this book about the coronavirus, I do what I always do when I write a book, I shut the door and prepare for uninterrupted focus on the research and writing task at hand. However, this time, when I turn on the orchestral *Beautiful Mind* soundtrack on Spotify, my focus is constantly being interrupted by Spotify letting me know of what steps they, as a company, are taking to combat the spread of the coronavirus.

During the past thirty days, as I have been researching and gathering the data for this book, I have been relentlessly interrupted by CNN, Fox News, Google, YouTube, Facebook, Spotify, the Weather Channel, that one store that I bought socks from once, and nearly every other business and platform with a relentless reminder of the dangers of the coronavirus pandemic. And when those platforms are not reminding me to be worried and to live in fear, the physical billboards that I see around town in route to the grocery store remind me to "WASH HANDS OFTEN WITH SOAP AND WATER FOR AT LEAST TWENTY SECONDS" to prevent the spread of COVID-19.

However, I can sincerely tell you that after I invested the 100-plus hours of time needed to gather the facts to write this book, I no longer experience any feelings of fear when I am interrupted by or alerted to the BREAKING NEWS related to the spread of COVID-19, which is why I am writing this book. I am writing this book so that YOU will no longer live in the perpetual fear caused by being pelted with an unrelenting barrage of social media posts, alarmist media headlines, and the rumors of somebody you know who knew somebody else who knew somebody who died as a result of "getting the coronavirus." Whether it is right-wing media, left-wing media, or your social media that is fueling the flames of fear, I know that many people, and even potentially you, are currently living in a constant state of fear. This book is going to provide you with the facts and information you need to be empowered to act as needed and to leave behind the emotions of fear that have preceded.

I'm going to cite stats for you, and I hope you realize EVERYTHING is cited with the "credible media sources" that also incite fear. The same media outlets feeding you the fear are also providing enough factual stats if you read between the lines. However, if you only actually read the headline of an article, you might miss that part.

Idleness truly is the devil's workshop, and many quarantined Americans are idle right now and are unsure of what to do with their down time. So, for the same reasons people like gossip and spreading rumors in the office break room, people who are now stuck at home are simply spewing their fact-free fears on Facebook and other social media platforms for all of the world to see. Whether it be for reasons that are either conscious or subconscious, many Americans are trying to pass the time by writing increasingly alarming posts which leads to more shares, online debates, and "social interacting" during this time of "social distancing" and "emotional distancing."

Ironically, in this world of constant digital connectivity, people were already feeling lonelier and more isolated than ever, even before the coronavirus panic. Think about the last time you went to a restaurant before the coronavirus shut most of them down. Were the people at the restaurant looking at each other or their smartphones? The start of being physically present but completely mentally absent began with the omnipresence of your smartphone.[1] Nielsen reports that now the "average" person is spending 11.3 hours per day consuming media.[2] The ability for fear to be spread virally via smartphones is new to us all. Consider this: in 2009, the "swine flu" infected 60.8 million American people and killed

12,469, but it did not cause the widespread panic and complete government shutdown of America.[3] Why? And why don't most people even remember the "swine flu" outbreak? Social media and smartphones were relatively new at the time of the outbreak, and I think this played a huge part in the lack of general hysteria.

I am writing this book for you, because as a husband, a father of five kids, an owner of multiple businesses, and the host of the chart-topping Thrivetime Show business podcast, I have literally interacted with thousands of people just like you over the phone, via email, and through social media who have become paralyzed by the fear caused by not knowing the facts related to the coronavirus panic. As I've lived my life, I've found that logic-killing fear is often related to not knowing the truth about the dangers we all face.

- In 1992, the NBA superstar basketball player Karl Malone refused to play basketball on the same basketball court as Magic Johnson for FEAR of getting HIV.
- The famous Greek philosopher Socrates was sentenced to death by hemlock poisoning in 399 B.C. for questioning the merits of the prevalent religion of the time for FEAR that

he would corrupt the youth and cause an end of the world as the Greeks knew it.

- Jesus was convicted of treason and was crucified at just the age of thirty-three for FEAR that he and his message would destroy the Roman empire.
- Many people ignorantly supported legal segregation for FEAR that African Americans would take jobs from non-African Americans and would ruin American life as they knew it.

FEAR is an unpleasant emotion that is caused by believing that the future is going to be worse than today, and something or someone is a direct threat to you or has the ability to hurt you. Fear kills joy, extinguishes hope, and reduces your ability to think logically. When you are wondering if a serial killer is in your basement, it makes it hard to sleep. When you are wondering if you forgot to turn off your oven, it's really hard to enjoy your beachside tropical vacation. When there is fear, there is no peace.

Now, before we go any further, I do have to make a big ask from you. Yes, I realize that we've just met, but could I have your undivided attention for the next two hours please? Pretend that reading this book is like going to your favorite theater (before the quarantine began) and you are being asked to turn your phone off or at least turn your phone onto airplane mode as you watch that feature presentation.

I promise if you will give me two hours of your time, I will give you some much-needed peace, hope, and maybe even joy as you realize how bad the coronavirus is and isn't. Throughout the course of this book, I promise that I will provide you the following panic-killing and fear-reducing benefits:

- You will no longer worry about who the virus can kill (because you will have the facts).
- You will no longer worry about the economic fall-out related to the coronavirus (because you will know the details related to our government's response).
- You will no longer feel the need to glue your face to your devices, sifting through the doomsday headlines and political agendas of either party to find the facts that you and your family need to be safe during this "weird time."
- You will no longer feel the need to debate with the soul-sucking, fear-mongering, end-times-prepping people on social media.
- You will find yourself 100 percent uninterested in going down the Google search black-hole of run-away conspiracy-theory research.
- You will take advantage of this downtime and

you will start crossing things off of your to-do list that you've been putting off because you previously "didn't have the time."

Recently, I interviewed Patrick J. McGinnis, who is a successful venture capitalist and the creator of the word FOMO, which stands for "Fear of Missing Out." Long before this coronavirus panic, the "Fear of Missing Out" became a HUGE problem for people in this world. It is a big part of the reason why we are addicted to our smartphones; we don't want to miss anything. Psychology Today now reports that the average person is interrupted over 100 times per day with smartphone notifications.[4] That's a lot of interruptions. So, while I do understand that just the act of turning off your smartphone long enough to invest the two hours needed to learn everything you need to know about COVID-19 could cause you to experience fear, I think it will cause less fear in the long run as we dismantle the panic surrounding the coronavirus.

You might be thinking: But what if I miss "the big call?" What if I miss the "big news update?" What if the supplier of the custom Darth Vader mask I ordered to protect myself from the coronavirus calls me to confirm my hat size? My friend, to make this deal fair, I promise you that I am going to write you one hell of a book that is filled with everything, and only everything, that you and your family will need to be able to live without fear during the time of this world-wide coronavirus panic.

# CHAPTER 1

# THE BOY WHO CRIED WOLF

*"If you tell a big enough lie and tell it frequently enough,
it will be believed."*
– ADOLF HITLER

*"Fear is the mind-killer."*
– ELON MUSK

How did we get into this situation? In late 2019, the world was introduced to a new version of an old disease, the coronavirus, or COVID-19 as it has come to be known. In the phrase COVID-19, the 'CO' stands for 'corona,' the 'VI' stands for 'virus,' and the 'D' stands for disease and 19 refers to the year it was recorded to have started. Whether it is coronavirus 4, coronavirus 8 or coronavirus 19, coronaviruses come from a large family of viruses that are common in people and many different species of animals, including camels, cattle, cats, and bats. While there has been debate over how this disease originated, we know COVID-19 originated in China, and for a while, it was little more than a story with few details reported infrequently by the mainstream media.

However, as America was going about its business and growing the economy at a record-setting rate, Neil Ferguson—the director of the Abdul Latif Jameel Institute for Disease and Emergency Analytics (J-IDEA), the head of the Department of Infectious Disease Epidemiology in the School of Public Health, and the Vice-Dean for Academic Development in the Faculty of Medicine, all at Imperial College, London— released a projection in February 2020 that would become the FEAR fuel that coronavirus pandemic panic needed to go viral on social media and traditional media. Neil Ferguson projected that 500,000 citizens of the United Kingdom population would die from this new disease and that the United States alone would experience a shocking 2.2 million deaths.

Once the world began to learn of Neil Ferguson's predictions, the right-wing and left-wing media fanned the flames of fear related to the pandemic panic and these headlines then turned into an all-out dumpster fire of panic as people began sharing these fears, and doomsday predictions on their personal social media accounts. Because the average person now spends over eleven hours a day consuming media on their smartphones, it only took hours for this coronavirus story to grow dangerously viral.

Quickly, people began to hoard toilet paper and essential food items in preparation for the "worst case scenarios" presented by Neil Ferguson. Why was toilet paper hoarded? Does the coronavirus cause diarrhea? No. But as a general rule, fear and panic kills humanity's ability to think critically. Try having a rational phone conversation with somebody while they are sprinting for their life in Spain's Running of the Bulls; it won't go well. Try teaching somebody about the merits of abstinence while they are currently engaged in having sex; it won't go well.

Without really knowing how the coronavirus would impact the amount of deaths in our country, our elected officials decided to let the fear of the unknown dictate their actions, beginning with Dr. Deborah Birx. Dr. Birx is the Coronavirus Response Coordinator for the White House Coronavirus Task Force; she is the one who called for the President to "shut it down."

The Governor or New York, Andrew Cuomo then stated during a press conference, "What we did was . . . we closed everything down. That was our public health strategy. Just close everything down. If you rethought that or had time to analyze that public health strategy, I don't know that you would say quarantine everyone . . . I don't even know that that was the best public health policy. Young people then quarantined with older people was probably not the best public health strategy because the younger people could have been exposing the older people to an infection . . ." [5]

Self-quarantining and shelter in place became mandatory and immediately Americans had all lost their constitutional rights to peaceably assemble in order to "keep you safe from the coronavirus." To make your life 3 percent easier, I have included the First Amendment from that controversial document that millions of brave men and women have fought to protect since September 17, 1787, "Congress shall make no law respecting an establishment of religion, or prohibiting the free exercise thereof; or abridging the freedom of speech, or of the press; or the right of the people peaceably to assemble, and to petition the government for a redress of grievances."

All of sudden, church congregations were not allowed to peaceably assemble, most Americans were forced to stay home and non-essential businesses were forced to close in order to "keep you safe." In states like Oklahoma, abortion clinics, liquor stores, and marijuana dispensaries were deemed to be "essential," while hair salons, retail stores, and other businesses were deemed to be "non-essential." Now, many Americans are forced to "stay at home" and wait indefinitely for this virus to run its course.

In Proverbs 16:27-29 the text reads, "Idle hands are the devil's workshop; idle lips are his mouthpiece. An evil man sows strife; gossip separates the best of friends. Wickedness loves company—and leads others into sin" (TLB). And that is exactly what idle Americans are doing. In fact, Newsweek reported that US alcohol sales increased by 55 percent in just one week amid the coronavirus pandemic lockdown.[6] And US News reported that the coronavirus pandemic has boosted marijuana sales while many businesses that are forced to be closed are struggling.[7] And when Americans are not out busy increasing their consumption of alcohol and marijuana, many have decided to invest their "free time," to post their pontifications about the coronavirus. In our digital world, it literally became impossible to turn on any media-serving device without being bombarded by the panic-filled headlines.

Only after things got out of hand and panic became the default setting of Americans everywhere did Neil Ferguson update his predictions. Neil adjusted his projections to predict that the coronavirus will cause 20,000 United Kingdom deaths, which means that Neil's early predictions were twenty-five times too high.[8] Oops. Ferguson's latest prediction of 20,000

United Kingdom deaths implicates that America should likely expect 88,000 deaths caused by the coronavirus—not 2.2 million deaths. To put this in perspective, America lost 80,000 people from the common flu in 2017-2018, and that number includes 180 children according to the Center for Disease Control.[9]

Let's take a moment to take in some facts. The coronavirus is twenty-five times less deadly than Neil Ferguson originally predicted. And according to University of California Berkeley Epidemiologist Dr. Arthur Reingold, "Children don't get very sick when they get the coronavirus . . . If they develop any symptoms at all they are mild, so severe illnesses and death are incredibly rare."[10] And according to the reports published by CNN, out of 731 confirmed and 1,412 suspected cases of COVID-19 in children in China, one child, a fourteen-year-old boy, died.[11] We now also know that 99 percent of those who actually died from the coronavirus in Italy were elderly and already had compromised immune systems.[12]

Since this "pandemic" began, I have received dozens of text messages, breaking news alerts, and emails full of COVID-19 propaganda. And I've talked to many frightened friends and family members who all believed that the end of the world is near; I can't even have a conversation them on a daily basis because fear is ruining their ability to think rationally.

President Franklin D. Roosevelt once famously said, "The only thing we have to fear is fear itself," and in today's current crisis he could not be more correct. However, I think his quote can only be outdone by Benjamin Franklin's famous quote, "Those who would give up essential Liberty, to purchase a little temporary Safety, deserve neither Liberty nor Safety."

# CHAPTER 2

# FEAR UNCHECKED
# BY FACTS

Because of the fear-mongering media, and the grossly overestimated reports from our good friend Neil Ferguson, we shut down our economy and forced "non-essential" businesses to shut their doors. This was a grave mistake (no pun intended) and the numbers below show why our leaders should have kept the world open for business. The only reason why our leaders closed the world was because of sheer public panic resulting from inflammatory, misleading, and alarmist reports by news organizations, as well as misinformation in the communications of our country's leadership with the public.

At the time President Trump issued the social distancing and other guidelines (March 16, 2020), the worst widely reported case for shutting the world down was the fear that there would be an estimated and predicted 510,000 deaths in the UK and some estimated and predicted 2.2 million deaths in the United States, as detailed in a report by the Imperial College. But we should ask ourselves, even if that happened, should the country shut down?

Fear unchecked by facts—that's the only reason why the country shut down. According to the CDC's data from 2017, one person dies every six seconds from the top ten leading causes of death.[13] Whether from heart disease, traffic accidents, medical malpractice, on average, 5,703 people die every day. This was all before the coronavirus, and irrespective of the coronavirus, we do not shut down local, citywide, regional, national, international, or world economies because of it. There is no reason to kill our economy by shutting it down solely based on these fears.

Why didn't our fearless leaders convey these facts while communicating with the public? This unchecked sensationalism comes with a real consequence: trillions of dollars in damages lost by small businesses and trillions of dollars in stimulus by the US government,[14] which already has $23 trillion in debt which grows by the second.[15] Not compelling? How about those killing themselves exceeding coronavirus death rates in some places.[16]

The fact is, there are different numbers, projections, click-bait stories, and "expert" opinions being shared every single day. The whiplash of the media and government is disorienting, and all the confusion causes more fear. Fear of the unknown, fear of leaving the house, fear of going back to work.

Here is a brief timeline of the coronavirus "pandemic" to show just how much things can change from one day to the next. Different leaders and experts are saying different things and giving misleading information, which is causing Americans to suffer.

**February 25, 2020**
*An expert in disease research said don't shut down the world for a virus.*
"I don't think the answer is shutting down the world to stop this virus. It's already out," said Michael Osterholm, director of the University of Minnesota's Center for Infectious Disease Research and Policy. Later in the article, Mr. Osterholm said: "trying to stop influenza-like transmission is like trying to stop the wind. It's virtually impossible . . ."[17]

**March 13, 2020**
*Epidemic experts predicted that up to 1.7 million US residents could die.*
The New York Times reported that officials from the Centers for Disease Control and Prevention and epidemic experts from around the world had gathered

on a conference call the previous month to explore worst-case scenarios for the coronavirus' toll.[18] The CDC modeled four scenarios and estimated that 200,000 to 1.7 million US residents could die.[19]

## March 16, 2020
*The White House task force started issuing social distancing guidelines.*
Birx herself referenced the British report at a coronavirus task force press briefing, where the Trump administration announced that it would issue more restrictive social distancing guidelines. Birx said the White House task force recommended limiting gatherings to fewer than ten people, consistent with the British report made public that same day. [20]

## March 19, 2020
*The "shelter in place" orders start.*
First in California, the government ordered residents to stay at home unless absolutely necessary (to go to the grocery store and other "essential" errands). Then more states follow suit.[21]

## March 24, 2020
*President Trump says we should never turn the country off.*
President Trump says: "Well, you have to make the

decision. Look, we lose thousands—I brought some numbers here. We lose thousands and thousands of people a year to the flu. We don't turn the country off—I mean, every year. Now, when I heard the number—you know we average 37,000 people a year. Can you believe that? And actually, this year we're having a bad flu season. But we lose thousands of people a year to the flu. We never turn the country off. We lose much more than that to automobile accidents. We didn't call up the automobile companies and say, 'Stop making cars. We don't want any cars anymore.' We have to get back to work."[22]

**March 26, 2020**
*The director of NIAID says overall consequences of COVID-19 will be akin to the flu.*
Fauci writes in the New England Journal of Medicine, "If one assumes that the number of asymptomatic or minimally symptomatic cases is several times as high as the number of reported cases, the case fatality rate may be considerably less than 1%. This suggests that the overall clinical consequences of COVID-19 may ultimately be more akin to those of a severe seasonal influenza (which has a case fatality rate of approximately 0.1%) or a pandemic influenza (similar to those in 1957 and 1968) rather than a disease similar to SARS or MERS, which have had

case fatality rates of 9 to 10% and 36%, respectively."[23]

**March 30, 2020**
*Trump has a "change of heart" and decides to keep containment measures in place.*
The New York Times reported, "The president's reversal on restoring normal life by Easter came as polling showed that voters overwhelmingly preferred to keep containment measures in place over sending people back to work prematurely." President Trump "was struck by the political surveying that indicated that the public wanted the restrictions to continue long enough to beat back the virus for fear that letting up too soon would simply reinvigorate the outbreak."[24]

\* \* \*

The honest truth is that the media and our leaders make matters worse by issuing misleading reports. With different reports and changes being made every day, it is hard to keep up with and concerning that no one seems to know what's going on. While headlines may be true and facts reported by the media may be true, they do not always tell the whole story, which puts the country at large into a panic, and the world economies at risk. Check out a few of these inflammatory headlines. When read out of context, these headlines leave readers panic-stricken. Why? Because a simple fact is missing: people in the US are dying at a rate of one person every six seconds anyway, regardless of the coronavirus. It's all relative!

- NY Post headline: "Coronavirus killing people in New York City at rate of one every 17 minutes"[25]
- Today.com headline: "Number of US coronavirus deaths now exceeds 9/11 death toll"[26]
- Foxnews.com headline: White House projects 100K to 240K coronavirus deaths as Trump tells US to prepare for 'very painful two weeks'[27]

Fear and panic are contagious. And the media is spreading fear to everyone. These headlines aren't communicating the facts; they're instilling fear. Now that you have seen the progression of the fear and panic that was created by the media, we need to ask ourselves a very important question. That question is "who is the coronavirus killing"?

# CHAPTER 3

# WHO IS ACTUALLY AT RISK?

As we take a look around at our country, we can clearly see that there is panic everywhere. From young to old, sick to healthy, there is a lot of widespread fear. I was at Walmart picking up several necessities this morning, and most of the people around me looked like they were doctors heading in for surgery. They had gloves, facemasks, and were sterilizing their grocery carts, literally from top to bottom. As we funneled into the store, everyone was looking around nervously, staying at least six feet away from one another. I was dressed in my standard clothing, absent gloves, a facemask, or any form of Lysol cleaner. You would have thought that I was the one that was dressed up funny. You should have seen the way that everyone looked at me—lots of judgement was passed.

What they probably didn't know was that I had just read an article discussing the coronavirus and personal protection equipment. According to the

CDC, "Most facemasks do not effectively filter small particles from the air and do not prevent leakage around the edge of the mask when the user inhales."[28] Facemasks are intended to be for people who currently have COVID-19 and can help to prevent others from catching the virus. However, they do not prevent people from getting the virus. While I do recommend caution when interacting with others, the level and irrationality of the precautions being taken is resulting in more fear than prevention. The common flu killed 80,000 people from 2017-2018, yet I don't see people wearing all of this equipment during flu season.[29]

When you take a look at the data and examine who is actually at risk for the coronavirus, you see a very clear picture. The coronavirus is most dangerous for people who are sixty-five and older or who have preexisting conditions. According to the Center for Disease Control, "older adults and people of any age who have serious underlying medical conditions might be at higher risk for severe illness from COVID-19." They go on to list several high-risk identifiers along with a list of the underlying conditions that could put people at a higher risk. Here is the actual list that is found on the CDC's website.[30]

Based on what we know now, those at high-risk for severe illness from COVID-19 are:

- People aged 65 years and older
- People who live in a nursing home or long-term care facility
- People of all ages with underlying medical conditions, particularly if not well controlled, including:

  - People with chronic lung disease or moderate to severe asthma
  - People who have serious heart conditions
  - People who are immunocompromised
  - Many conditions can cause a person to be immunocompromised, including cancer treatment, smoking, bone marrow or organ transplantation, immune deficiencies, poorly controlled HIV or AIDS, and prolonged use of corticosteroids and other immune weakening medications

- People with severe obesity (body mass index [BMI] of 40 or higher)
- People with diabetes
- People with chronic kidney disease

undergoing dialysis
• People with liver disease

If you are an individual that fits into one of those descriptions above, then you should absolutely take precautions to ensure that you do not get the virus. When you look at Italy's numbers and the statistics of who died from the virus, you get a very clear picture of who is at risk. According to Bloomberg, 99.2 percent of people that died in Italy from the coronavirus were older and had other illnesses. In fact, the average age of those that died was seventy-nine. All of the people who died under the age of forty had serious medical conditions. [31] Thus, the probability of someone under the age of sixty-five with normal health at risk of dying from the coronavirus is very low.

When you look at the statistics in the United States, it tells the same story. When you take an in depth look at the first 100 people who have died in the US from the coronavirus you see examples like:

• A ninety-year old resident of Sacramento County who had underlying health conditions and was in an assisted living facility
• A sixty-nine-year-old man from Bergen County who had a history of diabetes, hypertension, atrial fibrillation, gastrointestinal bleeding,

and emphysema
- A seventy-nine-year-old woman suffering from heart failure and lung disease before contracting the virus[32]

As of the day that I am writing this, according to Worldometer.com these are the statistics for deaths from the coronavirus.[33]

| AGE | DEATH RATE Confirmed Cases | DEATH RATE All Cases |
|---|---|---|
| 80+ years old | 21.9% | 14.8% |
| 70-79 years old | | 8.0% |
| 60-69 years old | | 3.6% |
| 50-59 years old | | 1.3% |
| 40-49 years old | | 0.4% |
| 30-39 years old | | 0.2% |
| 20-29 years old | | 0.2% |
| 10-19 years old | | 0.2% |
| 0-9 years old | | No fatalities |

Data obtained from Worldometer.com, last updated April 16, 2020

The graph clearly shows that your percentage chance of dying if you are sixty and above is significantly larger than if you are younger than sixty.

If you are a parent of a younger child who is nine years old and younger and you take a look at this data, then you should have great confidence to know that the likelihood that your child will die from the coronavirus is next to none. Yet, even with this data, people are afraid to even look at each other.

| PRE-EXISTING CONDITION | DEATH RATE Confirmed Cases | DEATH RATE All Cases |
|---|---|---|
| Cardiovascular disease | 13.2% | 10.5% |
| Diabetes | 9.2% | 7.3% |
| Chronic respiratory disease | 8.0% | 6.3% |
| Hypertension | 8.4% | 6.0% |
| Cancer | 7.6% | 5.6% |
| No pre-existing conditions | | 0.9% |

Data obtained from Worldometer.com, last updated April 16, 2020

If you have any of these conditions, then you have a much higher chance of dying than those that don't.

### Is the Coronavirus Actually Killing Kids?

There is a lot of fear concerning the safety and health of children, and the media feeds off this fear. As an example, CNN posted an article with the headline: '12-year-old girl with coronavirus is on a ventilator and fighting for her life.'[34] If you just looked at the headline, then you would assume that children are incredibly susceptible to the virus. This misleading headline would absolutely convince you that yes, we should shut down the entire economy and "save the kids!" But if you actually take the time to read it, you will see that the article talks about how this girl first contracted pneumonia, and then got coronavirus. Additionally, it goes on to say "Out of 731 confirmed and 1,412 suspected cases of COVID-19 in children in China, one child, a 14-year-old boy, died." If you take the time to watch the video, you will see that it clearly communicates that children do not need to worry about this virus.

Amongst all of the fear-inciting, speculated (and proven) misconstrued facts, and overblown headlines, there is one that sticks out the most. In China, only 0.2 percent of the total deaths from the coronavirus were children.[35] Experts agree, a low number of kids with the coronavirus are actually dying, in comparison to the seasonal flu (although numbers vary strain by strain, year by year).[36]

144 pediatric deaths were reported to the CDC from flu vulnerability this season of 2019-2020.[37] Maybe, we SHOULD all go ahead and shut down life and our economy ten months out of the twelve months each during to avoid our children getting the flu, or anything bad happening to them ever. Anyone

who is a parent would probably say that they wish they could shield their children from the bad. Yet most of us don't avoid taking them to school, soccer, dance, football, vacation, or anything fun because it requires driving in a car. If we are following the same logic that incited the coronavirus pandemic panic, we must never go anywhere or do anything ever again that could possibly be a risk. But the fact is, we don't do that folks. We never have and we never will back down from life just because of a little risk.

There is the legitimate precaution though with children and the coronavirus. Our little loved ones could—I repeat, COULD—pass the virus on to someone who is at a higher risk level such as the elderly or anyone with a compromised immune system. According to Dr. Fauci, "If a young individual, a child, gets infected, they may do perfectly well from a physical standpoint," he said, "but they may bring it home to a person who is susceptible."[38] Here's the thing though guys, don't we all do that anyway? I know for my family, I don't purposely bring them out to cough on the elderly or those with compromised immune systems whether they have the flu, another seasonal virus, or even the common cold. I have five kids. One thing I've learned is they are resilient. They may be carrying around the common cold 70 percent of the year. But that shouldn't stop them from doing activities and enjoying life, just because they are little carriers. Instead, I teach them to wash their hands and not cough on people.

### Are the Death Reports Accurate?

Even though the facts and reports hidden under the alarming headlines are continuing to make COVID-19 seem less and less serious and deadly, the country is still shut down and the fear of the general public is off the charts. When you see another report of a coronavirus death in the news, there are some things you need to know.

Even when a patient has other health concerns and complications, many healthcare workers are reporting the cause of death as COVID-19. When you see the reports of death in the news, the reporters aren't stating that the actual cause of death may in fact have been a heart problem or a kidney issue. Even if COVID-19 isn't confirmed but is "likely," healthcare workers are encouraged to list it as the cause of death. Here is what some leaders and experts are saying about the coronavirus death reports.

The Center for Disease Control's guidance on how to fill out death certificates is, "In cases where a definite diagnosis of COVID–19 cannot be made, but it is suspected or likely (e.g., the circumstances are compelling within a reasonable degree of certainty), it is acceptable to report COVID–19 on a death certificate as "probable" or "presumed." In these instances, certifiers should use their best clinical judgment in determining if a COVID–19 infection was likely. However, please note that testing for COVID-19 should be conducted whenever possible." [39]

Minnesota Senator Dr. Scott Jensen responded to the CDC's guidance, "In short, it's ridiculous. I spent some time earlier today just going through the CDC's (Center for Disease Control's) manual on how to complete death certificates. In that manual it talks of precision and specificity and that is what we were trained with. The determination of the cause of death is a big deal. It has an impact on estate planning. It has an impact on future generations and the idea we are going to allow people to massage and sort of game the numbers is a real issue because we are going to undermine trust. And right now as we see politicians doing things that are not necessarily motivated based on fact and science. The public's trust in politicians is already wearing thin. Any time healthcare intersects with dollars it gets awkward. Right now Medicare has determined that if you have a COVID-19 admission to the hospital you will get paid $13,000. If that COVID-19 patient goes on a ventilator you will be paid $39,000, three times as much." [40]

And Dr. Deborah Birx said, during a press

conference, "There are other countries that if you had a pre-existing condition . . . let's say a heart or kidney problem, some countries are recording that that as a heart issue or a kidney issue and not a COVID-19 death. Right now we're still recording it and . . . mark it as COVID-19 infection. The intent is right now that if someone dies with COVID-19 we are counting that."[41]

In short, even the reported deaths related to the coronavirus are questionable. We need to continue to look deeper than the headlines and realize that there are some hidden agendas behind the deaths being reported.

***

So, who is at risk of dying from the coronavirus? Short answer is people who are sixty-five years and older or who have preexisting conditions. If you fall into these categories then take extra precautions. If you do not, then you can set aside any fear you are experiencing and understand that you are much more likely to die from heart disease than coronavirus. Be smart. Don't go visit your grandparents during this time. But also don't give into the media's ploy to get you to click on their articles and be overcome by fear. We can get past this as a country, but we need to first start with the facts and realize that the overwhelming majority of people are not at risk for dying from the virus.

We cannot shut down our country due to people who MIGHT get the virus. If it were possible to keep our entire society safe at all times, I assure you most people would all be doing that for themselves and their children but that's not possible. We cannot shield our society, including our children, from any risk whatsoever. This type of fear-based logic restricts our children from socializing, living life, learning additional physical or mental skill sets, and so many other emotional, intellectual and physical benefits that daily social interaction provides.

A pandemic occurs when the mainstream media is telling you that a pandemic is upon us coming for our families. This creates soul-sucking fear if you do not know the facts. I'm here to teach you the facts, so you can protect your family and your children from this irrational, anti-logic-based fear created by our trusty government and media outlets (probably controlled by the government). Yes, we need a cure for the coronavirus, but we already have a cure for the hysterical fear that's running rampant: facts, logic, knowledge. Know the facts and let go of fear.

# CHAPTER 4

# IS THIS PANDEMIC TRULY "UNPRECEDENTED"?

Each and every single year, Americans face health threats such as colds, heart disease, cancer, the newest strain of influenza, and various other conditions or factors that could potentially be fatal. In fact, as stated earlier, the common flu killed 80,000 people in 2017-2018 alone.

Although 219 people die per day from the common flu, the media doesn't report on each and every case and death as though it was breaking news. However, with the coronavirus, the media feels the need to update you with this "breaking news." And because you are stuck at home quarantined indefinitely, many people feel the need to share these headlines and breaking news updates, and the "Doom Loop" cycle of the media writing alarming headlines that are then shared by social media users continues with seemingly no end in sight.

People fail to understand or are having a hard time admitting that this isn't the first pandemic the world has experienced. Everyone chooses to believe that this is the worst disease to have ever hit the planet, but the sad truth is that this is blatantly untrue. In fact, let's take a quick look at some of the biggest health scares to hit the human population in the last millennium that nobody seems to want to talk about. Let's also take one step further and look into the common daily causes of fatalities that are just as dangerous as a pandemic.

## The 1918 Spanish Flu

The 1918 influenza pandemic (also known as the Spanish Flu) was credited as the most severe pandemic in recent history before the coronavirus pandemic scare. In the span of one year, this particular strain of influenza managed to kill fifty-million people globally, with 650,000 deaths in the United States alone. Focusing on the US numbers alone, that puts the total fatality rate at 1,781 deaths per day. At the time of writing this, the coronavirus has killed 16,697 Americans. Following the same model that states that COVID-19 could possibly claim the lives of 100,000 Americans, that puts the daily average at 274 per day. This is not an optimistic number by any means; however, it's hard to say that this is the most aggressive pandemic ever when another virus historically outshines it.

### H1N1 (The Swine Flu)

The H1N1 strain of influenza was the next big thing in the world of pandemics. It actually originated in the United States and spread to the rest of the world. It came onto the scene between 2009 and 2010 and did a fine job terrifying parents, teachers, and anyone in the "at risk" population. Fun fact, the H1N1 influenza strain is actually a distant relative of the original Spanish Flu. Who knew? Well sadly, nobody because the facts were not made regularly available in news reports. From April 2009 to April 2010, the Center for Disease Control, or CDC, estimated there were 60.8 million cases of the swine flu, 274,304 hospitalizations, and 12,469 deaths in the United States alone. That means that on average 34.2 people died per day of the swine flu during this time period.

I remember friends and family members taking this very seriously, and it was a constant topic of conversation, but we never shut the country down because of it. The vast majority of those who got this new flu recovered and built up the necessary immunities to avoid it should it ever return. What's both funny and kind of shocking though is that if you ask a certain percentage of people who lived through the swine flu about their experience, more often than not they will have no idea what you're talking about. A pandemic almost completely forgotten.

## The West African Ebola Outbreak

Towards the beginning of 2014, the world started getting its first glimpses of the next flavor of pandemic: the West African Ebola Outbreak. On March 23, 2014, the World Health Organization began reporting cases of the Ebola Virus Disease, or EVD in the rural regions of southeastern Guinea. This officially marked the beginning of the West Africa Ebola epidemic. It was in fact the largest Ebola outbreak in history. However, it was the first time that many Americans were even hearing the word "Ebola." Media buzz began spreading fear as more and more stories regarding the virus started to surface. I remember there being a scandal at the Tulsa International Airport where unreliable sources claimed that a flight had been quarantined due to some passengers on the flight testing positive for the Ebola Virus. People were terrified of their insides becoming liquified, but at the end of the day, only a whopping eleven people were treated in the United States during the two-year run of this virus.

**The Common Flu**

Everyone in the entire world seems to be focusing on the projected death toll of COVID-19, but few are aware of the death toll that was the result of the common flu just one year prior. The common influenza strain managed to kill an estimated 80,000 Americans from 2017 to 2018. That's 219 Americans per day. Of the 80,000 that were lost to this disease, 180 of those deaths were children. An additional 959,000 were hospitalized on top of the death count. But do you know what the most alarming thing about this is? America didn't freak out! Americans got their flu shots and went on their way, but at no point did anyone suggest closing businesses or implementing social distancing. With a death count so extremely high, how do Americans not know the depth of lives lost during this time? Why was nobody freaking out?

**Additional Morbid Facts That Are Also Horrible but Never Focused On:**

In 2018, 250,000 patients died due to accidents in a hospital.[42] That's right, an "oopsie," a "whoops," a "my bad" managed to claim one quarter of a million lives and yet nobody banned doctors or hospital visits. Folks, an incredible 684 people die per day, every day from hospital mistakes and yet most people aren't overwhelmed by fear every time they go to the hospital.

In that very same year, deaths as the result of traffic accidents exceeded 40,000.[43] But people still get in their cars every day. In fact, over 4.7 million "death machines" were purchased that very year. Crazy right?

Heart disease, claims an average of 647,000 American lives each and every year.[44] That comes out to 1,772 deaths per day. Why aren't you filled with fear over your pending death soon to be caused by heart disease every time that you go out to eat?

\* \* \*

The sad truth is that we are currently living in a digital dystopia where people simply cannot seem to put their smartphones down. Remember, the average American spends over eleven hours consuming media in front of a screen of some kind each and every day. Push notifications interrupt us over eighty times in a given day as well. So, it is safe to say that the modern human being is extremely well connected to the world around them. However, this level of connection is also directly impacting our current situation.

We are living in the era of misleading headlines and published articles that are not fact checked and are filled with click bait. News stations keep a constant stream of bad news pumping through every possible form of communication, and our addiction to screens keeps us misinformed. The reason why the world didn't shut down during the Spanish Flu was due to the fact that nobody could get information instantly. The reason so many have forgotten about the swine flu is because social media wasn't quite explosive yet. And the reason nobody cares that the common flu had such a high death count is frankly because it's old news as far as diseases go. It's not sexy anymore. The coronavirus has such little proof behind it, which makes it easy for media outlets to capitalize on. The reach of social media and devices allows this fear to spread and further affect our current way of life.

So reading through all that you're probably thinking "well that's a lot of not-so-fun facts" but the point here is that throughout history, Americans have fought through adversity, trials, and tribulations. We have experienced MUCH worse throughout our history. We never have experienced the mass-produced fear that we are seeing now and we have never before forcibly shut our economy down.

Listing out other ways that people have died in recent history is not meant to instill more fear—quite the opposite. It's meant to show you that the mass hysteria over the coronavirus causing city-wide shutdowns is a media-fueled overreaction. Yes, it is serious, but are the measures being taken hurting more than helping? And will the fear and shutdown only end when there is a known cure?

# CHAPTER 5

# A REASON FOR HOPE

On April 8, the Institute for Health Metrics and Evaluation at the University of Washington, which had previously projected more than 90,000 American deaths from COVID-19, has now lowered its estimate on Wednesday to 60,415 deaths in the period until August 4, which means that the coronavirus is now less dangerous than the common flu which killed 80,000 people in 2017 and 2018 alone. Thus, quarantining our country and shuttering our businesses to hide from this virus makes about as much sense as euthanizing a person because they have a cancerous growth on their pinky finger. Nonetheless, until there is a cure, it's possible that every time there is another outbreak, social distancing measures might be put in place again. So, when will there be a cure?

On April 2, 2020, America got some great news from Dr. Stephen Smith who went on Laura Ingraham's show. He talked about the powers of the drug hydroxychloroquine and said, "I think this is the beginning of the end of the pandemic." Can an actual cure exist? A credible source is actually testing and providing facts about the cure. This is great news! But, before we get into that, let's find out who exactly Dr. Stephen Smith is. Let's make sure he actually knows a thing or two about pharmaceuticals, diseases, and a possible cure.

### Who is Dr. Stephen Smith?

Dr. Stephen Smith is an infectious disease expert who is the founder of The Smith Center for Infectious Diseases and Urban Health which is located in New Jersey. He went to both Duke University and Yale, and he started The Smith Center as a non-profit in order to address the different types of infectious diseases in the inner city, and originally had a focus on HIV cases. To clarify, this guy has the educational background from two of the most credible universities as well as the "boots on the ground," real-world experience to study infectious diseases. Additionally, Dr. Smith is a patent holder of two different patents. One of the patents he holds is a conditionally controlled attenuated HIV vaccine, which slows the rate of the HIV virus and weakens the effects.

Those are just a few of his accolades and accomplishments. The list goes on and on, but the point is that Dr. Smith knows what he is talking about. Now that we all understand that Dr. Smith is, in fact, a very intelligent human, we should rejoice about his findings of the treatment for the coronavirus with the drug hydroxychloroquine. He told Laura that out of all of his patients that had COVID-19, NONE of them that were on hydroxychloroquine had to be intubated (this means you need to have a ventilator due to failure of your respiratory system). THIS IS BIG. This means that the fight for ventilators might be over. If we focused on treating, testing, and scaling the hydroxychloroquine plan, not only could patients get better faster, but doctors could also treat them faster than ever and not worry about their limited supply of ventilators.

Even Dr. Oz piped in and said that he tested Dr. Steven Smith's discovery with sixty-two randomized patients who tested positive for COVID-19. The improvements in pneumonia alone were substantial. Without hydroxychloroquine, there was only a 54.8 percent improvement in pneumonia. When using the drug Dr. Oz reports an 80.6 percent improvement in only five days of using hydroxychloroquine. The results speak for themselves.

So you might be wondering what the deal is. We have a cure, or something closer to a cure, so why are we still in isolation? If you are just an average American with five kids like myself, you probably haven't attempted to get a drug FDA approved too many times in your lifetime. Unless of course you have, in which case you already know the facts here. But, it's important to know and understand the drug approval process. According to the Federal Drug Administration, there is a two-tiered system of approving new drugs to the marketplace; there's the *Standard Review*, and then there is the *Priority Review*.[45]

The *Standard Review* is for the drugs offering only minor improvements over other therapies. The *Priority Review*, would be something a little bit closer to what our friend here, Dr. Steven Smith, is concerned with. A *Priority Review*, best case scenario, is typically completed in six months. Here's the thing folks, we need the cure now, not in six months.

There is a fast track option though. According to the FDA, when the urgency is there, the fast track program can get a drug approved within sixty days.[46] This is great news for anyone thinking the lack of a cure will keep us all living in fear and quarantine for six more months. And since Hydroxychloroquine Sulfate is actually already an FDA approved prescription for existing treatment options and therapy for other diseases, it should be approved without a hitch.[47]

This is phenomenal news that needs to be shared with the world so that everyone can not only know about it, but maybe we can stop living in so much fear. Fear is the real killer in this pandemic, and the more and more information that we can get out to calm and dispel the fear, the faster we can get our country back to normal and start working again. The sooner we get our businesses open, the sooner we Make America Work Again, and the sooner we can get our economy back up and going and return to life as normal. It's time now to begin taking strides toward making our economy better.

# CHAPTER 6

# THE WINNERS AND LOSERS
# OF THE SHUTDOWN

Winning and losing is an interesting concept. Why do we have to speak in such black and white terms? Is there enough room in a conversation regarding winning and losing to simply be content to play the game? Why is this concept of winning and losing so closely tied to our view of how the world works? When a company makes more money, are they winning? When a company is forced out of business by another company, are they losing? Did they deserve to lose? Did they play the game incorrectly? Did they misunderstand the rules of the game, or were they simply bad at it? Why are we tying the making of money to winning?

These questions fascinate me, because I find money vastly misunderstood in the current day and time that we live in. I want to take a look at what I will consider to be winners and losers as it relates to companies making more or less money during the coronavirus economic shutdown. And while I do not want to inflame a political conversation, I think there is an underlying winner and loser that is going unnoticed in this conversation that will ultimately cause a significantly higher level of pain than the coronavirus and a temporary economic shutdown.

Before I look at some companies that will make a significant amount of money during this economic shutdown or highlight some companies that will lose greatly, I think it's valuable to take a second and define what money is. I would put forth the opinion that in the current climate, there is very little that people are willing to define, much less fully understand so that their words or concepts can be clearly defined. Money is one of those concepts. But I find it rare that someone truly understands what money actually is, or what it represents. In Ayn Rand's book *Atlas Shrugged*, a character by the name of Francisco d'Anconia puts forth a monologue that, in my opinion, is a clear and defensible position on the purpose, value, and definition of money. Francisco finds himself essentially taking up the defense of money, denying that money, in and of itself, is the root of all evil. Francisco asks an interesting question, "Have you ever asked what is the root of money?"

Francisco continues, "Money is a tool of exchange, which can't exist unless there are goods produced and men able to produce them. Money is the material shape of the principle that men who wish to deal with one another must deal by trade and give value for value. Money is not the tool of the moochers, who claim your product by tears, or of the looters, who take it from you by force. Money is made possible only by the men who produce. Is this what you consider evil?

"It is not the moochers or the looters who give value to money . . . Those pieces of paper . . . are a token of honor—your claim upon the energy of the men who produce. Your wallet is your statement of hope that somewhere in the world around you there are men who will not default on that moral principle which is the root of money. Is this what you consider evil?"

Now his speech is quite long, and I encourage you to read it in its entirety, but now you will know where I am coming from when I distinguish which companies are winners and losers amidst the coronavirus pandemic. As we look at the companies' efforts to navigate changing economic conditions, government actions, and public opinion, we will see that they are either rewarded with an increase in revenue or penalized by a decrease in revenue.

\* \* \*

The media and a seemingly unending stream of government officials are issuing order after order for people to shelter in place, stay at home, and not go outside.[48] This forces people to consume products and services that can be delivered to their home resulting in an increase in sales for companies that use a delivery service or the internet to fulfill orders.

According to Quantum Metric, a data analysis firm that analyzed the traffic of 5.5 billion visitors to online and mobile retail websites from January 1 through the end of February, online sales have shot through the roof.[49] Quantum Metric looked at data acquired from last year and this year, and saw a massive jump in sales from people buying products and services from brick-and-mortar companies. Specifically, Quantum Metric saw a jump of 52 percent in online sales when compared to the same time frame a year ago.

Another interesting statistic is the total number of shoppers also increased by 8.8 percent since this coronavirus craziness began. This is in reference to one of the hardest numbers to move in the world of ecommerce, which is the conversion rate. The conversion rate is the number of people that have to visit your website in order to make one sale. So for instance, if it took 100 people visiting a website that sold shoes to sell one pair of shoes, your conversion rate would be 1 percent. The cool thing about knowing this number is that if you want to sell ten pairs of shoes, then you simply have to send ten times the amount of traffic to your website, and according to your conversion rate, you will have a high statistical probability of selling ten pairs of shoes. Now companies were not doing anything significantly different to their websites this year compared to last year that we could attribute this increase in sales, which indicates that an outside force, such as the fear of venturing outside the home, is having an almost 9 percent increase in the number of people buying online.

Now, if there was a single company that was literally made for a coronavirus economy, it is Amazon. They invest heavily in supply chain, logistics, and they place a high value on the customer experience which drives them to innovate their systems and deliver products to your door as fast as possible. In many places, delivery can happen the same day a purchase was made. When I was growing up, if you wanted to buy a computer, you would physically go to a computer store to look at all of the new technology. You would have to go and look at the massive speakers and TVs at Circuit City or drool over the shiny computer cases with the cool LED lights at CompUSA. And you would have to trust your gut and the salesman to know which brand and product to purchase.

But there has been a shift in the personality of the modern consumer away from risk and towards convenience. The modern consumer does not want to risk buying something and have that item turn out to be something less than the best, or less than they expected. A contributing factor to the rise of Amazon's success has been the video distribution platforms like YouTube. When a person wants a new pair of headphones, they used to have to go to a store and make a decision on which pair to purchase based on packaging, and the recommendation of the sales representative that is following them around the store. Now, you can go watch an unboxing video on YouTube and listen to a person review fifteen different brands and types of headphones, subject the products to hilarious stress tests, and ultimately give you their recommendation. You can then click on their affiliate link to the product on Amazon, read the customer reviews and testimonials about the product, and then have the product on your doorstep in less than twelve hours. And since people are being sent home, and are more and more comfortable working from home, this trend will only increase.

The coronavirus outbreak has only reinforced consumers' proclivity toward online shopping. The pandemic has forced many businesses to shut down their storefronts and to direct their customers to their website as much as humanly possible. People are scared to go outside as news agencies continue to drown them in worst-case, fear-induced scenarios related to the spread of the coronavirus, so the only way they can buy products is by using online stores.

Amazon owns the e-commerce market. 38.7 percent of all US e-commerce sales flows to Amazon according to eMarketer.[50] Did you know that during February 2020, that people visited Amazon.com over 2 billion times? There are 2,419,200 seconds during the month of February which means that if you divide the number of times people visit Amazon.com by the number of seconds during the month of February, you get over 830 visits per second.

Amazon knows how to react quickly to market changes. For example, Amazon expanded its fulfillment center staff by hiring 100,000 people and increased the hourly wage across the board by 2 percent as of March 16, 2020.[51] Now while sales are up, traffic is up, visitors are up, the question is: what does this mean for Amazon revenues? Can Amazon convert an increase in demand and sales into an increase in revenue?

The market is underestimating the coronavirus impact on Amazon. Amazon is also suspending or deprioritizing the fulfillment and processing of products that they have deemed as not necessary. Amazon has temporarily suspended its "Fulfillment by Amazon" shipment program according to TechCrunch.com.[52] Another area of concern for Amazon is although necessary items are in more demand, consumer spending as a whole is trending down according to a survey completed by Moody's Analytics.[53] So even though we are conditioned to use Amazon for everything AND they are deemed as an essential business, they too are being impacted.

One sector that historically experiences its most growth during down economies is the Information Technology Services sector of the economy. This sector is made up of companies that support the technology needs of businesses as opposed to those companies hiring local staff to complete those support tasks.

During a down economy, or an economy where businesses tighten their belts, close locations, lay off staff, and reduce expenses, one of the largest areas of expense for a business owner is their payroll. During a down economy, a business owner still needs to keep its technology up and running smoothly, but can no longer afford to pay a staff of two or three people to keep that technology running, so they begin to reach out to what is called a Managed Services Provider, or MSP. A MSP will take over all of the technology support needs of a business owner and responsibilities of the former staff, but they can complete these duties for around half of the total salary expense of in-house staff. A managed services provider, or IT company, can also complete these support tasks at a much faster rate thus reducing downtime and resolution times for their clients because they typically have many more people on staff than the small business owner could afford to employ.

A down economy creates more of a push of clients to an IT company, as opposed to marketing having to pull them into the sale. Technology Solutions Consulting Inc, an IT and Managed Services company started by Josh Fellman and M. Jerome Garrett, was started during the last recession in 2008 and proceeded to grow rapidly during that down economy and went on to become one of the larger IT companies within its market.

Whether it's e-commerce or IT companies, there are some notable winners in this shutdown. So who is losing in this coronavirus economy? Nearly every small business owner and their staff is being hurt by the coronavirus economic shutdown which has unemployed 16,000,000 million Americans as of the time of the writing of this book (April 9). Many businesses deemed "non-essential" have been forced to close their doors due to the coronavirus. This includes retail stores, hair salons and barbershops, restaurants and bars, and more. While some businesses have attempted to survive by allowing their employees to work from home, it is not working and it is not sustainable. The level of "half-assery" going on caused by allowing America's workers to work in their distraction-filled homes with little to no accountability is tremendous. Businesses are losing. Big time. Even businesses that don't have to shut down entirely are affected by lack of revenue; and nearly every American business is reducing hours, laying off employees, and figuring out how to make things work during this two-month experiment with communism. Employees are actually being paid not to work, everyone is getting a paycheck from the government (The Paycheck Protection Program), and our state and federal government gets to decide which industries are essential and which ones are not.

In an effort to be safe and precautious, we have put many people in danger and have compromised our values as a nation. Our entire economy has been required to shut down. Now this raises an interesting question: would you rather have safety or freedom? The United States was built on the prioritization of freedom over safety. Of course we want safety, but not at the expense of a great deal of freedom. As

Patrick Henry said in 1775, ""Give me liberty, or give me death!"

With the number of shelter at home orders, business closing directives, and executive orders of governors, mayors, and city managers telling people where to go, when they are allowed to be outside their homes, I can't help but wonder if the real loser in this economy is our freedoms, and the winner is government in the amount of control they are allowed over our lives and businesses. As George Washington said, "Government is not reason. It is not eloquence. It is force. And like fire, it is a dangerous servant and a fearful master."[54]

# CHAPTER 7

# A CURE WORSE THAN
# THE PROBLEM

Dr. Fauci, the nation's top infectious disease expert, estimated on March 29 that COVID-19 could kill between 100,000 to 200,000 Americans.[55] This would translate to 306 to 611 deaths per million people in the United States. At face value, this estimate would understandably compel most doctors to tighten physical distancing initiatives. Ask any successful business owner how they feel about the economic shut down, and see what they say. Most of them will tell you how ridiculous it is that we cannot be working during this "pandemic" regardless of the "danger." Why do so many successful entrepreneurs reject the extreme social distancing measures being implemented? Is it that entrepreneur's value monetary gain over human life? Or does the entrepreneurial perspective allow them to see the true human cost over the long term?

Let's start with the question: Why the hell would anyone listen to an entrepreneur instead of a doctor anyways? To dig into this issue, let's look at some stats on entrepreneurship. About 16 million or 4.9 percent of the United States is self-employed.[56] We also know that 96 percent of businesses will fail within ten years[57] and that only 30 percent of businesses have five employees or more.[58] Thus, the percentage of the population who has been in business for ten years of more and has grown a company to more than four employees is 0.06% (0.049 x 0.040 x 0.300); in other words, roughly one in every 1,700 people in the US is a successful business owner.

Let's compare that to the 1.1 million doctors in the United States. 0.34 percent of the population or roughly one in every 300 people in the US is a doctor.[59] Now, does this mean successful entrepreneurs are smarter than doctors? I'm sure most entrepreneurs would readily admit that their book smart memorization skills range from "only if I must" to "couldn't memorize if my life depended on it." The list of accomplished entrepreneurs from Bill Gates, to myself, to Walt Disney who didn't graduate from college is long and illustrious, and none of us could have made it as doctors, due to our inability to sit still, memorize, and follow procedures. One of the original dropouts, when questioned on his inability to memorize, said it best:

> *"If I should really WANT to answer the foolish question you have just asked, or any of the other questions you have been asking me, let me remind you that I have a row of electric push-buttons on my desk, and by pushing the right button, I can summon to my aid men who can answer ANY question I desire to ask concerning the business to which I am devoting most of my efforts. Now, will you kindly tell me, WHY I should clutter up my mind with general knowledge, for the purpose of being able to answer questions, when I have men around me who can supply any knowledge I require?"*
>
> *– Henry Ford*

I'm sure most entrepreneurs would be fully satisfied in conceding the IQ test to the doctors. However, most successful entrepreneurs have simply found a way to pull together readily available "ordinary" information from multiple sources to achieve "extraordinary" results. The answer to why this mindset is so rare is likely rooted in conventional education. Conventional education often gives multiple choice tests where one answer is right and three are wrong. In business, there is rarely one definitively right answer but rather multiple options, each having various pros and cons. They teach us in school that there are clearly defined rules, but in business, we rarely find complete clarity in regulations and are often forced to deal with conflicting regulations.

In school, they teach us to reach consensus—vanilla decisions that semi-please everyone. However, the market tends to reward bold actions. Most importantly, in school, we are taught to get a job and seek immediate payment. Yet entrepreneurial success is largely dependent upon thoughtful risk taking and delayed gratification. Entrepreneurs are not looking for success in the short term, they are looking for long term success. They are normally playing chess not checkers. My friends, what this means is that it's not surprising that entrepreneurs would be less swayed from groupthink and would be more likely to offer a dissenting opinion on the COVID-19 lockdown strategy. How does a pragmatic entrepreneur look at the COVID-19 issue? Let's look at how Canada's top CPA, Josh Spurrell, started advising Canadian entrepreneurs on this issue.

First off, he became frustrated when public releases lacked any numerical context. Press conference after press conference simply presented two vague graphs, one with a high apex protruding the dotted line of the hospital capacity and one with a flat apex below the dotted line of the hospital capacity. None of the graphs included the number of cases requiring an ICU bed, the number of ICU beds available, or the number of days of the pandemic. Facing a similar medical challenge in Canada, he began digging for data. Using data from other countries, he estimated the number of expected simultaneous serious cases. Like Henry Ford, he then pulls in ordinary data from other sources. He found historical articles detailing the number of ICU beds in the country. Ultimately arriving at the conclusion that there would be approximately 478 deaths per million people in Canada, putting his projection smack dab in the middle of Dr. Fauci's projection of 306 to 611 deaths per million people. Entrepreneurs when faced with uncertainty often dig for data. However, entrepreneurs are not satisfied with the just short-term projections and because entrepreneurs are playing chess not checkers, they question what happens after the apex?

Well, the most comparable economic event happened in the "Great Recession" of 2008 and

2009. Most people are well aware of the economic carnage that occurred, but what about the human cost? I don't mean esoteric feelings; I mean cold, hard, undeniably data of the human cost of the "Great Recession." According to Forbes, the United States suffered 4,750 excess suicide deaths after the recession hit in 2008. Although horrific, this number will likely pale in comparison to the deaths we should expect from the COVID-19 economic fallout after the pandemic passes. Surprisingly, suicides are the least of our concern.

The New York Post noted that researchers found that the "Great Recession" was tied to an additional 263,000 cancer deaths in wealthy Organization for Economic Co-operation and Development (OECD) countries such as the United States, Canada, Australia, and the UK.[60] The OECD has just over 1.3 billion people.[61] which means that the rate of additional cancer deaths attributable to the "Great Recession" can be pegged at 202 deaths per million. Why does this occur? After a significant economic contraction, budgetary cuts will be made. As shown by the multi-country study with varying healthcare systems, there will be less dollars for both private and public healthcare systems. Still, 202 deaths per million are less than the COVID-19 deaths predicted by Dr. Fauci. If only I was not burdened by the forward-looking entrepreneur mindset, I would be able to stop there. However, I have to dig deeper. Cancer normally causes 1,831 deaths per million people in the United States, which means an additional 202 deaths per million is an increase of 11 percent in the cancer death rate.[62] It is illogical to estimate that only cancer treatment will suffer with budgetary healthcare constraints. We should consider the following list of other top ailments in its entirety:

1. Heart disease: 1,978 deaths per million
2. Respiratory disease: 489 deaths per million
3. Stroke: 447 deaths per million
4. Alzheimer's: 371 deaths per million
5. Diabetes: 255 deaths per million
6. Influenza: 170 deaths per million
7. Kidney disease: 154 deaths per million

TOTAL (INCLUDING CANCER)– 5,695 DEATHS PER MILLION

We should realistically expect that reduced healthcare funds will likely increase all of the major issues by 11 percent. In other words, a significant economic contraction similar to the Great Recession is likely to increase deaths by 626 deaths per million or a total of 204,827 people in the United States. This is above the upper end projections for COVID-19 in the United States.

The further we get into this lockdown the more likely a depression-type economic scenario exists. Many feel that the economic contraction due to the COVID-19 shutdown will exceed the effects of the "Great Recession" and may rival the Great Depression of the 1930's.[63] My friends, the likelihood of the economic slowdown resulting in more than 204,000 deaths become more probable each day the shutdowns continue.

Doctors are on the front lines of this battle, I get it. However, just like any war, the generals need to make the call with a 30,000-foot view. Imagine a battlefield where the front-line soldiers peer off into the distance to see a formidable opponent. Meeting them head on will certainly result in casualties. Understandably, the infantry on the front lines wants to take the long way around the forest and flank the enemy from the rear. However, the generals must have the resolve to see the minefield around the forest and order the troops to march forward and face the battle head on. This is what has to happen in this coronavirus war. War's messy, but the simple truth is: the shutdown will kill more people than COVID-19.

# CHAPTER 8

# WHEN IT BECAME UNETHICAL TO GO TO WORK

It's easy to read a book and shrug off the contents of it as an excuse to not actually take action, so I wanted to provide you with some ACTUAL stories from ACTUAL business owners on how the economic shutdown has affected them in their own words.

**Aaron Antis,** *Shaw Homes*

We have been in business for thirty-five years and have experienced record years in sales in 2016, 2017, 2018, and 2019. Sales have been on the incline for the last four years as the economy under Trump has been booming. The problem is that the amount of money required to keep a business this size going is substantial.

However, when government interference closes our entire nation and will not allow ready, willing, and able buyers to even leave their homes, how can our business even have a chance? There are many buyers who we have been speaking with who have decided to stay home even though they need to move. How can someone come visit our homes when the news is threatening that our leaders in government are going to ticket and potentially jail our potential clients for leaving their homes to come visit us?

While we are at a financial standstill due to a national shutdown, the interest clock doesn't stop ticking. Let's take a minute to look at the financial responsibilities that we have committed to that we are not being given the freedom to pursue in a free market. One model home has a monthly cost of $2,500-3,000. Multiply that times twenty-two and you get a $60,500 cost to operate empty model homes. Each of our 550 plus lots cost $200-300 per month in interest. That totals $137,500 in interest on lots that we can't sell without customers coming in to look at them.

With 192 homes under contract and under construction for buyers waiting for us to build their dream home, we have opened up Construction Loans in good faith to build homes built to order for people who aren't allowed to work right now. With many of our buyers missing their paychecks and potentially missing payments on their bills, this could lead to lower credit scores and defaults on credit to be able to close on the homes we are building for them. For every customer that defaults during a build, that creates another home that stays on the back of Shaw Homes to finance until it is sold. Each one of those homes that defaults costs us $2,000-3,000 per month. If half of the 192 homes under construction were to default, that would add another $240,000 of debt for our company to carry monthly.

Meanwhile, the fear that has been propagated by our media and government employees is the real pandemic. All of our employees are terrified to leave their homes. We have employees in their mid-thirties with young children that are scared to come to work because they fear for their children's lives, even though statistically, children are largely unaffected by the virus.

We are allowing the government to force people to stay home. I ask that our leaders in government get a clue and reopen America immediately. Quit crushing our nation's job producers with the overarching policies that are putting unfair burdens on businesses by forcing America to stay home in an unprecedented lockdown of the nation known for and founded on FREEDOM.

## Terry Wren, *America's Best Event Photography*

They say that "all things happen for a reason." I'm not sure the reason for COVID-19 or for closing the entire United States of America during the virus, but I do know this: I am praying every day that my business will be able to recover when we do open back up for business. At the time of me writing this, we have thirty more days to go before we even know if we can get back to work or if there will be another extension on the shelter in place.

I am the owner of America's Best Event Photography in Fort Worth, Texas. We are the largest youth sports photography company in the area and we service leagues in the north Texas area and Waco area. We have been in business for over twenty-seven years doing youth sports and preschool photography. Our business is seasonal and we make the majority of our operating income during eight weeks in the spring and eight weeks in the fall. At the beginning of the year, we signed up so much new business, mainly baseball accounts, that I knew that we were going into our most profitable and best baseball season ever!

Then, two weeks before our opening day, disaster struck. I was hearing something about a virus. I was paying attention but not really that much because I thought, "we have had viruses before and we get over them." Fast forward two weeks from that thought and I went from making a steady income to making zero money. I went from having ten full-time employees that made my business run to having to lay every one of them off on a Sunday night. I remember making that dreaded phone call to each of them and it felt like a knife being slashed through my heart. Never in all the years of being a small business owner had I ever had to lay off a full-time employee. As days turned in to weeks, I came to the realization that having any baseball season was probably slim to none. Now here is where it really gets bad. We work double shifts in the spring and fall seasons and we make our income for the entire year in those months, and I knew that if I didn't have a spring season that I would not be able to bring back any of my employees in the summer. In the past, every August I would say to my bookkeeper, "I cannot believe I was able to keep everything going the entire summer." And at the exact time the bank account was running on empty, it was time for the fall football season to start, and we were back up and running.

I'm a believer and I know God will take care of me. I have a roof over my head and food on my table, but I know that I had ten employees that I've always taken responsibility for some of whom live paycheck to paycheck and don't know where their next meal is going to come from or how they are going to pay their bills. As for me, I stay prayerful that this will end soon and everything will go back to normal and that somehow, I will be able to pay the bills. I do know one thing: I will NEVER take for granted the simple things in life, and I will NEVER complain about having to go to work ever again.

## Gabe Salinas, *Window Ninjas*

Window Ninjas is a window and pressure cleaning company that operates in four states and eleven locations. We are a force in North Carolina, South Carolina, Virginia, and Tennessee and have been growing since our inception in December 2017.

We have faced time off due to hurricanes hitting our corporate office in Wilmington, North Carolina on multiple occasions. Our Nashville office has been affected by tornados, and all of our locations suffered through the ice and snow storm that kept us locked in for weeks during the winter of 2018. We have continued to grow and take these setbacks in stride and keep moving forward. In fact, we were up at least 25 percent in some markets and as much as 750 percent in other locations! All while never looking for help or a hand or any interference from the government or our local elected officials. Something we are quite proud of!

Since the start of this COVID-19 crisis in January of 2020, our world has been turned upside down. Our company's employees are fearful and in a completely different mindset that we never imagined we would see. We do weekly group employee interviews and have a hiring process that only allows the best of the best to be able to work with Window Ninjas. We are constantly looking to hire excellent employees, which is a big part of why we are growing in a manner that is unprecedented for a company that is so young.

Our customers are generally older individuals

who are retired and are middle to upper-middle class or considered wealthy. They are the type of people that see the value in maintenance and upkeep and desire to have services provided on their time. Since the COVID-19 issue, we have had extensive conversations with them and they are more concerned about us being safe than wanting our services to be completed.

On the other hand, our employees, aged from twenty-one to thirty, are more worried about not being around anyone, not interacting with anyone, and sheltering on the couch. They are spewing false data and clearly do not comprehend the factual information provided by the Center for Disease Control's website. Employees that were once great are now lackluster and ordinary—two things that we steer clear of as a company. We are driven to be exceptional!

The effect COVID-19 has had on our business is troubling, to say the least. We are extremely concerned and have had to reduce staff and cut hours because of the fear that is fed to us daily from the news media and government officials. Their acknowledged mistakes and disinformation they have fed to the American people have made things very difficult for us. We are taking things day by day, making adjustments constantly, and following the CDC recommendations on how to keep our employees safe and our customers safe. We want our employees back to full time and we really want their old attitude and outlook back. We also don't want to spend all of our savings on a hope and a prayer that the Federal Government may or may not give us reimbursement for paying our employees to do nothing.

## Jamie Fagel, *Jameson Fine Cabinetry*

After thirty-five years in the cabinet industry and two recessions—the first being in 1992 in Canada, which led me to the United States, and the second recession being in 2007- 2008 in the US—I started my own cabinet company. How hard could it be right? Family owned and operated—a business with little money. But I didn't have to travel anymore and I could finally be at home with my family.

The business was started in the front room of our house. Then we expanded and moved to the basement of my son's house. We all continued to work endless hours and did anything and everything to keep things moving and customers happy. We expanded again into our current place;

this time we have a showroom and a shop. We look like a real company. Everything was lining up and the three years of grinding it out was finally getting us somewhere.

Then, the virus hit. We are now in survival mode, wondering what to do. How long can we survive this? If we do not have the same revenue coming in, what customers will we lose now and in the future? Do I still try to sell retail which only made up 40 percent of my business? How do I get new builders? I have so many questions that even with thirty-five years in the building and cabinet industry, I didn't have an answer for any of them.

It's been approximately two weeks since the virus became a physical obstacle now in our way. Like any entrepreneur, we have a problem. We look at how to get around it, under it, over it, through it. We need to keep moving. Our retail business is now at zero revenue. We still have a few projects that we are trying to finish up, but we run into more obstacles because of the virus every day. I hope our company survives. I'm fifty-six years old and will lose everything. I don't think I have another start-up in me. I just keep repeating to myself: this too will pass.

## Kevin Thomas, *Multi-Clean Janitorial Services*

Twenty-seven years, yes, that's how long I have been in business. My entire adult life, my commercial cleaning business is all that I have known. And now, in the matter of a few weeks, that could possibly be all gone due to a virus that is barely making a dent in the health of America. So far, my company has been forced to lay off over 100 hard-working individuals due to an unrealized fear of the coronavirus.

As the government has decided to continue to force businesses to close, this in turn has directly affected my company, Multi-Clean, the availability to create revenue to pay my employees.

The great fearmonger, the mainstream media, has created and perpetuated fear. Unfortunately, there are millions of people in our country who follow and believe the media, and allow this fear to be the fuel for the panic engine across America.

Hospitals in my own city of Tulsa, Oklahoma are cutting hours of the staff and having to lay off nurses and medical workers. This makes no sense at all. Where are all the sick people the news is telling us about?

Most of our employees literally live paycheck to paycheck. How do I explain to my employees that we just don't have money to pay you right now? The only panic that our employees have is the panic of not being able to pay their electric bill or providing enough food for their family. I believe that the struggle here is not the actual coronavirus but the political correctness, and the insane idea that this shutdown is a good idea for our country.

So my question to the government is: at what point does the economy take precedence over a virus that kills less people than the common flu virus every year? Someone needs to step up and say enough is enough. We all need to practice safe distancing, wash our hands, and get back to work.

## Josh Wilson, *Living Water Irrigation*

It is Tuesday evening, March 24. I am sitting at my kitchen table with my wife. The conversation begins slowly.

Finally, I ask the question, "Honey, how long can we make it on zero revenue?" Silence, dead silence. This woman who believes in me with all of her heart, the amazing woman that allowed me to begin this journey, the very same woman who has supported me through long days and sleepless nights, my partner in this ride, she says, "I don't know!"

Whenever I talk about the effect that COVID-19 has on my life, on my business, it is wrapped up in that one conversation. I have had this conversation so many times at this point that I feel like it is rehearsed. "Josh, are we gonna make it through this?" "Josh, am I gonna be able to keep my job?" "Josh, are we still working?" "Josh, how do you remain so positive?"

If they only knew, if they only knew what is running through my head, the thoughts, the concerns, the worry.

Then, I snap back. Then, I remember that God is still on the throne. I remember Matthew 6. Then, I know that I am His. I know that He has brought us this far and He will never leave or forsake me. Yes, the coronavirus has affected our business. Yes, it has affected our lives. But also, it has made my faith stronger; it has brought to the forefront the importance of community, the value of relationship, and ultimately, it has brought Christ back into the conversation.

Living Water Irrigation will press on, we will not fold, we will do our best to serve our community and keep our people employed. Our number one focus is people, always has been, always will be. We will be stronger and better!

## Nathan Sevrinus, *Complete Carpet*

This is the first time in my forty-plus years that I have seen something affect the American people's lives in a way that takes away their hope. Even after 9/11, we all gathered together; we gave each other hope and kept the country going. This coronavirus is a tipping point for everyone I know.

Did you get swept away with the tidal wave of news saying the sky was falling, hide in your homes until it blows over? Or did you stand up with a voice of hope and fight. I had to figure out who I was as a father to give hope to my kids. I had to learn what kind of husband I needed to be to give hope to my wife. I was tasked with being a boss and father to my employees to restore their hope. And finally I had to choose what kind of business owner my customers needed to be able to have hope in this "time of crisis." I needed to receive hope also to be able to give it.

I learned quickly I could not rely on any news sources to give me hope, because they all wanted to quarantine everyone and hide from the virus. If that worked, then the virus wouldn't have left China and spread to 140-plus counties. So I needed another source of hope. I found it in a business podcast called "The Thrivetime Show." Every day they were breaking down the actual numbers compared to the hype. They exposed the insane steps we were taking to combat the virus, "This is like burning down your home to kill a mouse in the house." They gave real time advice to business owners for what to do next. They empowered us with comparisons that no one else was making, like H1N1 was as bad or worse then and we didn't shut down the county.

As a boss and owner of a carpet cleaning business, I had to give my employees hope every day. Because every day, the world we live in changes. One day, we needed to socially distance. The next day, we could only gather in groups of fifty or less. The next day, all entertainment venues closed down. The next day, all non-essential businesses were told to close. Each day it was a different kind of fear and loss of hope my employees had questions about. I had to make sure that I had that hope before the day started and had an answer before the question was asked so they could follow my confidence each day.

As owners of a business, my wife and I were

tasked with how we message our customers in this time of falling skies. How do we bring hope to our customers without spreading fear? This is a very fine line to walk, because if I go all out in my message about how we are combating the coronavirus, then I am adding to the fear because people will see our message and say, "See, even the carpet cleaning guy is scared." But in this political climate, there are those that say if you are not doing enough, they will call the authorities to make you respond to the pandemic.

Each job I went on I met great people who were struggling to keep living a normal life. I discovered that I needed to bring hope also to every customer I got to serve. One lady told me that I was the very first person to visit her in over a week; my heart broke. I started searching out hope, trying to find it. In the fear and darkness, I did see great people step up and try to be that hope.

I'll end with this. As a Christian, this is the first time I've ever had the government tell me that I cannot meet at church. Maybe I'm old school, but I really believe that we are to lay our hands on the sick, and they will recover. Maybe that means instant healing or maybe we heal their heart because not only are they sick but no one is willing to go near them. Isolation I think is as damaging as any sickness because you feel like you've been abandoned. Only a few people have the power inside themselves to have hope in the midst of darkness by themselves. That is why I had to step up and start giving hope to everyone I meet. My kids need to know I have a plan and that they will be safe and secure in the months and years to come. My employees needed hope that they could pay their bills and not be unemployed. My wife needed a single source of comfort to battle the tidal wave of social and news media beating the drum every day that the "sky is falling." We all need to start writing pay-it-forward checks of hope to everyone we meet, because someday we will need someone to write us a check in return.

\* \* \*

These are just a few of the HUNDREDS of letters I have gotten. If you are a small business owner, check out Appendix A to figure out how to get the money that you need to stay afloat during this time.

My friends, hopefully by now you are starting to see why we must take a stand against the over-hyping and fear-spreading gossip related to this disease. The real war is not with the coronavirus, it is with the misinformation that we are being fed. It is with the government that is trying to (not that shrewdly) hide behind the fear to take away our rights, our liberties, and everything that made this country great. This country was built on dedication, hard work, and the American dream. This country was built on the idea that the harder you work, the further you get ahead. We cannot stand by and watch everything that our forefathers fought and died for (more than have currently died from the coronavirus (6,800)) go to waste on the promises of a government bailout.[64]

This country was built on work, has grown to its greatness on work, and so, we NEED TO RETURN TO WORK! It is time for us to stop being led blindly by the politicians that are feeding us lies about the coronavirus being so much more than the common flu. It is time to stop listening to our friends and family about why we must stay home and shut down our businesses "for the greater good." It is time to open our doors again and start providing the great service to our customers that they have come to expect. It is time to get the economy going again; to create jobs, income, and wealth; and get back to doing the one thing that we know how to do best which is WORK.

# CHAPTER 9:

# THE ROOT OF
# THE PROBLEM

We've talked about the facts of the virus, the misleading information, the grossly overestimated predictions, the unnecessary precautions people are making. We've talked about the result that the misinformation has had on society, how the government-mandated shutdown is destroying the economy and the lives of business owners and their employees everywhere. All over something less deadly than the flu. So how did we get here? Why is it that, this time, the world is shutting down unlike ever before in modern history?

Remember earlier when we talked about the swine flu of 2009 that infected over 60 million Americans and killed 12,469 people? Like most Americans in 2009, you probably were only vaguely aware of it. In fact, everyone that I talk to about it seems to remember hearing about it, but did not personally experience any fear or develop key memories from that time. The swine flu "epidemic" was just another virus in the series of viruses that have impacted this earth throughout history.

The swine flu killed thousands of Americans and infected millions more. The CDC estimates that from April 12, 2009 to April 10, 2010, there were 60.8 million people that were infected and 12,469 deaths in the United States alone. 274,304 people were hospitalized during this time as well. The CDC even estimates that as many at 575,400 people may have died from this virus across the world. 80 percent of those deaths occurred in people who were younger than sixty-five years old. This is actually very different from a typical flu-like virus. Typically, influenza deaths occur predominantly in people sixty-five years and older. There were plenty of opportunities for the country to have the "excuses" needed to shut down and take away our civil liberties in the name of public health, but that didn't happen. Why wasn't there a freak-out in our country? What is so different about the coronavirus that has everyone freaking out about catching it? The answer: social media.

During the present coronavirus situation, the media is sensationalizing the deaths of younger people, even though 99.2 percent of the people that the coronavirus kills are people who are elderly or have preexisting conditions. Why didn't our country shut down for the H1N1 virus, that was predominately killing people younger than sixty years old, and it *has* shut down for the coronavirus that is doing the opposite? Could there be another agenda at play? The truth is that there is a huge problem in our country that is having a devastating impact, and I am not referring to the coronavirus. The media perpetuates fear, and in doing so, has done significant damage to our great nation. It isn't the virus that is killing the economy, it's the fear of the virus that is killing the economy.

All you have to do is look on Facebook or turn on CNN and you will quickly recognize what I am talking about. If you look up headlines today, you will see articles like "Coronavirus Live Updates: Grim Models Project High US Toll in Months-Long Crisis"[65] or "Live updates: More people have died in the US from the coronavirus than in the 9/11 attacks."[66] Almost all the headlines in the news communicate a bleak and hopeless future, perpetuating fear and giving lawmakers more power to take away our liberties and keep us locked in our homes.

*Time Magazine* has taken a stab at discussing how social media is impacting our fears and response to the coronavirus.[67] They talk about how "social media platforms like Facebook and Twitter, which didn't exist or barely existed during past major outbreaks, are facilitating important conversations about the virus, while at the same time allowing sensationalism and misinformation to spread." Back in 2009, when the H1N1 was running rampant, people were not spending over eleven hours per day entrenched by media. That, combined with the fact that pretty much anyone that is alive can get a social media account and therefore has some level of a platform to spout their opinions, definitely has contributed to the perpetual fear that Americans have of the coronavirus. The intensely negative bend that the media has towards this situation plus the constant exposure to these negative perspectives is an unbeatable recipe for fear.

A big question to ask is why the media consistently produces content that is bent towards the negative? The reason is pretty simple and obvious if you think about it. It's all about those clicks baby! Sex sells, fear sells; extreme statements get the attention of the average consumer. In this media and information saturated world, in order to increase engagement with posts, videos, articles, etc., you have to do something to grab people's attention. Unfortunately, good news doesn't get nearly as many views as bad news.[68] A BBC article about this talks about a "negativity bias," which is a psychologist term for our collective hunger to hear and remember bad news.[69] Most, if not all, people are addicted to negative or fearful information. The article reports that, "In lab experiments, flash the word 'cancer,' 'bomb,' or 'war' up at someone and they can hit a button in response quicker than if that word is 'baby,' 'smile,' or 'fun' (despite these pleasant words being slightly more common). We are also able to recognize negative words faster than positive words, and even tell that a word is going to be unpleasant before we can tell exactly what the word is going to be." It doesn't matter who you are, most people are wired for the negative.

Negativity being the default for most people combined with the truth that most people, according to Forbes, don't change, it is not surprising that, as a culture, we allow this negative bend of the media to perpetuate.[70] Most people that I talk to recognize their need to get off social media, put down the burger, exercise a little, work harder, etc. But they don't actually make the changes. According to Forbes, one of the reasons for this is because people don't know how to sustain motivation. While the average American might try every once and a while to stay away from negative news, if they don't have that strong internal motivation, then they will go right back to it. Just like water flowing downhill, people like to take the path of least resistance.

Unfortunately, when our natural tendencies take us to the negative, the path of least resistance is to continue to live addicted to that negativity.

In becoming addicted to our phones, we have become a negativity and fear driven culture which is why, unlike during the swine flu, the majority of people are endorsing the course of shutting down our country. The probability of the average person dying of the coronavirus, even in worst case predictions, is 0.0007 percent.[71] People are afraid of a virus that is far less likely to kill them than an accident, cancer, or heart disease according to the CDC.[72] Shutting down the economy for a virus that is allowing fear to drive decision making is not the path we should take. Let's learn from H1N1; we will get through this. Let's not destroy our economy and country in the process.

# CHAPTER 10:

# THE CURE FOR FEAR

In a time where we can stay constantly updated with the latest news developments, where our friends are traveling to, or what our favorite cultural icons are up to, we must ask ourselves, "Has social media, which began as a fun or easy way to stay connected with our friends and family, now become a destructive force in our daily lives?" In this chapter, I will break this down like James Brown.

We all have anecdotal examples of how social media has had a negative impact on our lives here and there. At one point or another, most of us have become victims of epic political Facebook clashes, the mindless ten-minute scroll on Instagram, or the vortex of Twitter. When dealing with social media in these regards, the solutions are simple. We know not to get into arguments on Facebook because it typically causes the other person to become even more entrenched and committed to their views that differ from ours. Deep down, we know there are a thousand better ways to spend our time than scrolling through Instagram without thinking. If we're honest with ourselves, we understand that perhaps reading 280 characters at a time on Twitter isn't the best way to understand complex issues. Solving these social media issues are simple, but do we really understand the deeper negative repercussions this can have on our lives?

How many people have you met who are proactively trying to become dumb? Seriously ask yourself: is there anyone you know that is legitimately working to lower their intelligence, memory, and overall mental cognition? At first thought, this question obviously seems absurd. With the advent of cognitive training apps such as Lumosity and Elevate, we would likely think that generally speaking people are trying to become more informed and intelligent. Unfortunately, through the abundant use of social media on our smart phones, we are becoming dumber.

According to Dr. Ron Friedman, social psychologist and contributor to *Psychology Today* magazine who specializes in human motivation, studies show that the "mere presence of a cell phone—even when it's not being used—influences people's performance on complex mental tasks."[73] The study asked its participants to quickly identify two numbers in a row of digits that would equal a pre-specified total (as in which two numbers that added together equal a total of six). Half of the participants were asked to keep their phones on their desk, the other half were asked to put their phones away. Even though not a single phone went off during the experiment, participants that had their phones on the desk performed nearly 20 percent worse than those that had their phones put away. Again, there were no notifications, alerts, or rings going off for the people that had their phones on the desk. If these participants performed 20 percent worse WITHOUT the interruptions of notifications, just with the presence of a phone, imagine how our performance declines even more if we have notifications for our social media turned on!

Another negative impact of social media is its ability to induce sadness and contribute towards less life satisfaction through constant use. In her Forbes article, Senior Forbes Contributor Alice G. Walton references a study performed by the Hubert Curien Pluridisciplinary Institute out of the University of Strasbourg in France that found that moment-to-moment happiness and life satisfaction declines through social media use.[74] The study would survey eighty-two different people five times a day for fourteen days to assess their happiness and life satisfaction after using Facebook.[75] The experiment found that the more people used Facebook, the less happy and satisfied they became. Researchers also found that when the participants interacted with other people directly in person, happiness and life satisfaction were not affected. The study concluded that while Facebook seems to fulfill the basic human need for connection, Facebook actually did the exact opposite: it made people feel sad, dissatisfied, and alone.

Despite knowing how social media and smartphone use can decrease our mental abilities as well as how social media can negatively impact our emotional state, perhaps you're still not convinced? If these reasons aren't compelling enough, then let's examine what a massive waste of time social media can be. In an article by Carolyn Sun, published by Entrepreneur magazine, it was determined that the average person will spend more than FIVE YEARS of their life on social media.[76]

Carolyn's article continues to explain another terrifying conclusion this study found—the average person will spend only one year and three months over their entire life socializing with friends and family in real life. We will spend five times more of our life interacting with people digitally than in real life. Your daily routine of proving people wrong on Facebook or endlessly scrolling through Instagram isn't looking as tempting now, huh?

CNN Health partnered with child development experts to do a study on the amount of time teenagers spend on social media.[77] The study had over 200 eight graders participate from eight different schools across six different states throughout the country. These students (and their parents) allowed the researchers to register their Instagram, Twitter, and Facebook profiles to an electronic archiving company CNN contracted. Over a six-month period, these researchers analyzed 150,000 social media posts. The study found that the more teens use their social media accounts, the more distressed they could become and found that the heaviest social media culprits checked their feeds more than 100 times per day. CNN Health also reported that the average teenager's daily time spent on social media is more than their time spent sleeping or in school—a whopping nine hours![78]

Naval Ravikant, a major Twitter investor and co-founder/former-CEO of AngelList, sums up the dangers of social media best with this quote, "I don't think modern science has good answers here. I think that the modern world is actually really bad. The modern world is full of distractions. Things like Twitter and Facebook are not making you happy. They are making you unhappy. You are essentially playing a game that's created by the creators of those systems, and yes, it can be a useful game once in a blue moon. You are engaging in the dispute, and resentment, comparison, jealousy, anger about things that frankly just don't matter."

One of the most destructive traits related to social media that we have all experienced at one time or another is the vicious attacks that seem to happen so quickly when we try to stand up for our values on social media. Want to update your Facebook status on your stance against abortion? Prepare for a tidal wave of hate, vitriol, and negativity to fill your comment feed. Do you dare tweet about how the world might be overreacting to the coronavirus pandemic just a little bit? I've seen responses where numerous people will call you an evil, anti-Christian, murderer.

We now live in an age where people are more concerned about appearing right to the masses on social media rather than actually holding an established set of core values by which they live their lives and make decisions. In the liberal media, conservatives are often portrayed as intolerant, uneducated, and racist bigots, which then influences the way people act on social media. While the left often self-righteously prides themselves on standing up for the rights of those who are mistreated in society, it seems they hypocritically mistreat others while advocating for their views.

I recently did an incredible interview with best-selling author Mark Manson on the chart-topping podcast The Thrivetime Show.[79] During the show, I asked Mark to break down why people reject good values in our world of political correctness. His response was on point:

> *"We simply aren't aware of our values. I think part of it is just all the distraction from all the technology and phones and blah, blah, blah. We become so caught up in just this autopilot that we don't even realize what our priorities are a lot of the time. Then I think the second thing that happens a lot, and I think this is driven primarily by social media, is that we like to portray certain values perhaps online, or to each other, that we don't necessarily live or embody or act in our real lives. I think the problem is the media environment in general is rewarding that right now. It's rewarding self-righteousness and moral outrage. It promotes that behavior and that attitude towards people. I think the right has had its own dose of that in the last ten years, but I think right now it's the left's turn to really, really just scold*

*everybody as if they're everybody's mother or something like that."*

What I hear Mark saying here is that people are willing to operate within a flexible morality—a morality that changes based upon how we feel in the moment. People are more concerned with being socially validated for what they believe, than actually believing in anything at all. If we disagree with what someone says on social media, it's now socially acceptable to say a myriad of hurtful and false things in order to destroy that person's character and reputation publicly. The worst part about all of it? It's acceptable to not only operate this way, but if what you say is hurtful enough, you'll get "likes" for it.

Because of the world that we live in, constantly plugged into social media, it is no wonder that the fear of the coronavirus spread like . . . well, a virus. People who have done literally zero research on the topic automatically get to become so-called experts and share articles that have a headline that they think proves their point BUT THEY NEVER EVEN READ IT. To help fight this, I have provided some action steps that you can take to stop surrounding yourself with fear and negativity.

**Action Steps to Take TODAY:**

## 1. Delete all social media apps

What action steps should you take right now to cure the disease and destruction of social media addiction? The first and frankly most powerful yet simple step is to delete all of those gosh darn motherloving social media apps. Try a wild experiment today: delete all of your social media apps. All of them. Don't even think about it, just do. If you think too much about it, your mind will try to justify why you need to keep them or perhaps, you'll create reasons why social media doesn't negatively impact you, but just try it for just one day. At the end of the day, ask yourself, "What did I really miss?" I believe you'll find out that the answer is frankly, "You didn't miss much." In fact, you'll find that your days are so much more fulfilling, productive, and purposeful by not being a slave to your social media.

## 2. Turn off your notifications

As a business coach who has worked with hundreds of companies across the nation, one of my biggest pet peeves is to hear clients say, "I don't have enough time." It's an excuse that's easy to use, but is simply not true. You do have the time, you just haven't taken the right actions. You always have time for what's important if you know how to organize this time. A practical action step you can take right now to free up your time is to turn off all of your notifications. If you are struggling to find time to get the important things done, you'll find that getting rid of the constant distractions of notifications will help you create HOURS of more time. By not having your notifications turned on, you'll also forget to check your social media accounts and stop the incessant cycle of mindlessly being on your social media.

### 3. Put your phone away when getting stuff done

The last simple action step that can dramatically help your productivity and overall happiness is putting your phone away when getting stuff done. While performing work for your customers or trying to knock out a big project, studies have shown that if you have your phone near you, your mental cognition will decrease by 20 percent. This can lead to countless problems: making errors on your work, creating costly mistakes on projects, and being mentally absent with customers that are paying for 100 percent of you. Increase your happiness, save time, stand up for what's right, and get off of your phone.

If you put your phone away, I can promise you two things and those are: First, you will find yourself getting much more done, and second, the world will not cease to rotate while you are doing it. It is okay to turn your phone on airplane mode and get stuff done.

### 4. Look past the alarming headlines
Even if you take all these steps, the fact of the matter is, a lot of other people won't. So in a sense, you will still be surrounded by fearmongers. When you inevitably see an alarming headline about coronavirus and the state of the world, look past the panic. Read the article, then go deeper and look at the citations referenced in the article. Read articles through the lens of knowing that the media profits from your fear and hysteria; fear is contagious, but digging deeper and educating yourself will keep you immune.

If more people were more passionate about finding the truth and facts about the coronavirus than just trying to share a pithy headline, maybe, just maybe, we wouldn't find ourselves clamoring for the government to bail us out.

# CONCLUSION

*"Freedom is never more than one generation away*
*from extinction. We didn't pass it to our children in the*
*bloodstream. It must be fought for, protected, and handed*
*on for them to do the same."*
– PRESIDENT RONALD REAGAN

As a country, our combined overreaction and panic-filled responses to the virus on social media has now given our local, state and federal elected officials our implied consent to violate our Constitutional and First Amendment right to "peaceably assemble" anytime that they choose to do. You were told that you couldn't go to church "for your safety." You might have been told that you couldn't go to work "for your safety," and your personal liberty was certainly imposed upon by your state or local government "for your safety." And although one of the most notable Founding Fathers, Benjamin Franklin once famously warned us to never be willing to give up our personal liberty in exchange for "a little temporary safety" we did just that with the lack of caution and common sense that is typical of mob rule.

When Benjamin Franklin wrote, "Those who would give up essential Liberty, to purchase a little temporary safety, deserve neither liberty nor safety," he wasn't joking around or sarcastically speaking. He was being both serious and direct with the Americans of the time—and with you. He was warning you that ANYONE WHO WOULD GIVE UP ESSENTIAL LIBERTY TO PURCHASE A LITTLE TEMPORARY SAFETY DESERVES NEITHER LIBERTY NOR SAFETY. Yet, as a country we have now set the very dangerous precedent that we, as Americans, are willing to give up nearly all of our essential liberties for even just "potential temporary safety" from a virus that a non-American Director of a Saudi Arabian-backed institute predicted might possibly cost 2.2 million American lives.

During the coronavirus panic, we now have provided corrupt politicians, aspiring dictators, and those who do not have your best interests in mind the proven plan and the blueprint for how to shut our economy down and to convince the vast majority of Americans to willingly give over their essential liberty that countless American soldiers have died to protect. It has now been proven that the next time another potential panic, crisis, or potential crisis presents itself that every American now has a platform (whether they earned it or not) called social media that can be used to virally spread panic and fear. And once Americans are scared, they begin to skim the headlines and go light on the facts and heavy on spreading their panic-filled feelings on social media.

When our Founding Fathers signed the Constitution, they didn't include an addendum to the First Amendment that read, "Congress shall make no law respecting an establishment of religion, or prohibiting the free exercise thereof; or abridging the freedom of speech, or of the press; or the right of the people peaceably to assemble, and to petition the Government for a redress of grievances . . . unless we believe that a report being produced by organizations that don't have our best interests in mind are telling us we should shut down." (Neil Ferguson is the Director of the Abdul Latif Jameel Institute for Disease and Emergency Analytics which was founded by the Saudi Arabian named Mohammed Abdul Latif Jameel, whose home country Saudi Arabia we are currently engaged in an oil-price war with).

I want you to ask yourself the following question with passionate enthusiasm. Why are we referring to this as COVID-19 and not COVID-18 or COVID-12? The truth of the matter is this is not the first time a "new" or "novel" strain of a coronavirus has impacted the planet and the people living on it. You see on this great planet, there are unfortunately many different types of human coronaviruses and some of which cause minimal upper-respiratory tract illnesses. However, COVID-19 is a new "novel" disease that has previously not been seen in humans on our planet up to this point. However, with previous scares we did not shut our great country down. And as a response to the 2009 swine flu that infected 60.8 million Americans according to the Center for Disease Control we did not shut America down either. But with COVID-19, we did shut it down. And we shut it down without really even knowing what COVID-19 means, how many people it was going to kill, and why we were so panicked to begin with.

Personally, I am unsettled by the Director of the National Institute of Allergy and Infectious Diseases, Dr. Anthony Fauci's comments of, "we have to be prepared when the infections start to rear their heads again . . ." I am mentioning this because we are going to have another new "novel" virus that is going to scare us next year. The sooner that you and I can come to grips with the fact that even the common flu (that mass-media currently hasn't decided to turn into an endless breaking-news cycle) killed 80,000 Americans in 2017 and 2018 alone. You and I must resolve in our minds that we shall never again allow our hard-fought-for American rights to be stripped away under the guise of "safety." In order to not lose our essential liberties, you must be aware of them and be willing to stand up for them and to fight for them. You and I must both step up and fight back against those that would wish to strip us of our essential liberties in the name of keeping us safe.

We have to understand we are going to get hit with another "COVID-19" type virus, and when we do we have to make the decision to not allow FEAR to dictate our actions and control our lives. The next time something scary happens, we must commit to getting off of social media and into the act of gathering the facts. We must refuse to sob and join the ignorant mob. We must simply hit pause long enough to gather the facts before we decide on how we are going to act. We cannot allow our freedoms to so easily be stripped away from us as we did this time. We must stand up for something or we will be willing to fall for anything. Moving forward, we must invest the time needed to appropriately UNMASK the fear, the fear-mongering social media posts and the panic-producing mainstream media which now specializes in serving up scary headlines. As the fear and panic related to the coronavirus panic subsides, we are now left to deal with the real results of government's over-reaction to the coronavirus. It's sad, but think about how much we have let this COVID-19 panic to truly impact us as Americans:

- Without a bullet being fired by our enemies, we gave up our Constitutional rights to peaceably assemble. We allowed ourselves to essentially be put under house arrest and "grounded" by our states' governors without committing a crime. And without amending our constitution, we made it illegal and immoral to go to work and to attend church.
- Without surrendering as a result of a takeover from a hostile government, we allowed foreign organizations to tell Americans how we should react (including the World Health Organization and the Abdul Latif Jameel Institute for Disease and Emergency Analytics).
- Without a vote being taken or a law being passed, 16,000,000 Americans lost their jobs as of April 9, 2020.
- In order to slow the spread of the coronavirus, you were forced to pay for the public school that your kids were not allowed to attend while the teachers still get paid. And you can no longer take your kids to the public parks which you are forced to pay for with your tax dollars.
- As a result of the coronavirus-mandated shutdown of large portions of the economy,

many business owners were forced to get a government loan in order to survive (The Paycheck Protection Program and the Economic Injury Disaster Loans and Loan Advance).

- Take away a man's pride and you increase the chances of a man's suicide. The national hotline providing emergency help to people suffering from emotional distress has received nearly nine times more calls than it did this time last year, with tens of thousands of Americans reaching out for assistance amid the coronavirus crisis, according to U.S. officials.[80]

- As a result of our response to the coronavirus and our local, state and federal government's obsession with quarantining ourselves at home, alcoholic beverage sales shot up 55% according to both CNN and Newsweek.[81]

- In order to limit the spread of the coronavirus every student has now been forced to miss out on ¼ of their school year. This means that every American student has now had to sacrifice 1/48 of their formal education to limit the spread of the coronavirus that has been shown time and time again to be less lethal than the common flu to kids, adults and nearly everyone other than those who have an already severely compromised immune system.[82]

• The scare of the coronavirus combined with the government shutdowns, quarantines and "safer at home" orders has created a tremendous decline in the number of overall patients visiting medical facilities and thus American healthcare professionals are being laid off,[83] furloughed and cut by the thousands as the revenues of medical facilities plummet to historic lows.[84]

• The coronavirus costs $6.2 trillion of government spending and is likely to cause inflation.

In order for us all to move forward with our lives and to live without fear in a social media and mainstream world that is still buzzing with coronavirus conspiracy theories, and predictions of the next pandemic that could quickly cripple us again, we must be able to quickly recap the facts that both caused and paused the coronavirus panic and logically come to the decision that there is nothing to fear, except the panic itself.

**The virus is killing less people than the flu.**

**The shutdown will harm more people than the**

**virus will.**

**The headlines aren't telling the whole truth.**

Due to the fear-induced media hysteria, we are being fed misinformation about the virus and its effects. This is causing irrational actions to be taken such as shutting down cities and issuing shelter-in-place orders. The economy, and therefore the American people, will suffer more from the "temporary" closing of businesses than we will from the virus. And the culprit that is causing the mass-produced hysteria? The media—news outlets, celebrities, social media. Fear is spread faster due to our addiction to our phones and our proclivity towards fear—and the media feeds into that and profits off of it.

The cure for this pandemic of ignorance is educating yourself with the facts. Headlines often misconstrue facts; look deeper. Press in to figure out what is ACTUALLY going on. Don't buy into fear—it will cost you more than you know.

Fear kills joy, extinguishes hope, and reduces your ability to think logically. We have to get back to normal, to do what we do best which is work, and it all starts with knowing the FACTS, which are the only thing that kills FEAR.

So what now? Unmasking fear starts with you. It starts with informing yourself of the truth and then informing your family. It starts with looking deeper than the attention-grabbing headlines. Yes, fear is contagious, but so is confidence. If you exude confidence in the truth, you will successfully unmask fear.

# APPENDIX A

# GUIDE FOR SMALL BUSINESS OWNERS: HOW TO GET MONEY BACK INTO YOUR HANDS

Unless you are still living under a rock while reading this book, you've probably heard about the 2.2 trillion-dollar Cares Act relief bill that was passed on Friday, March 27.[85] This relief bill was passed in hope of cushioning the blow of the economic destruction caused by the coronavirus pandemic and to help the small business owners with their finances. These funds will be distributed through the Small Business Administration (SBA). Small businesses are allocated $600 billion dollars through this package.

This bill allows small business owners to borrow up to two million dollars and receive two and half months of payroll. Sounds pretty good right? This will be the lifeline you need as a small business owner to get through this crazy time. So how do you actually get this money into your hands? First let's dive into what options are available to you.

### 1. Paycheck Protection Program (PPP)

This is the loan that will be given to business owners in order to cover the cost of their payroll for two and half months! This amount is determined by taking the employer's average payroll cost from February 15, 2019 to June 30, 2019—being capped at 10 million dollars. The best part? This loan is automatically forgiven, meaning that you do not need to repay this loan in any way shape or form as long as your workers remain employed. It is also retroactive as far back as February 15, so that employees who have already been laid off are able to be brought back onto a company's payroll.

Keep in mind that the money given to you from the Payroll Protection Program must be used to pay your employees. That money is not there for you to remodel your kitchen or buy a new work truck.

**To apply for PPP:**
1. Go to your local SBA Approved bank make sure that you are working with 7A lending

program.[86]

2. Shortly after you contact your banker you should be given an application to fill it out. You will need to provide the following documents:

- 2019 – 941 quarterly payroll reports
- 2020 – 941 quarterly payroll reports for the first quarter of 2020
- Proof of lease payment
- Proof of utilities
- Signed copies of your tax returns
- Personal identification
- Articles of organization
- And bonus, you don't have to put up any collateral! That means you do not need to provide proof of assets

## 2. *Economic Injury Disaster Loan (EID)*

This is the loan that business owners can apply for. They can apply for up to two million in capital loans with an interest rate of 3.75 percent. This loan is there to help provide financial relief to business owners who are experiencing a decrease in revenue due to the coronavirus lockdowns.

**To apply for EID:**
1. Go online to SBA.gov and fill out the application.[87] This form will ask you a series of questions pertaining to your business, and you, the business owner.
2. Fill it out and FOLLOW UP

*If you're curious about qualifications, you are deemed eligible if you are any of the following:*
1. Any business concern, nonprofit organization, veteran's organization, or Tribal business concern that employs no more than 500 employees (or the size standard in number of employees established by the Administration for the industry in which such business operates)
2. Sole Proprietors
3. Independent Contractors
4. Self-Employed Individuals

If you are on the fence about if you would qualify or not, go ahead and apply. The worst thing that could happen is that you would get denied. The same goes for any business owners that have been lucky enough to be deemed "essential." This coronavirus pandemic may not seem to have a huge effect on you or your business at the moment, but it is still a very good idea to go ahead and apply. Firstly, the money awarded through the Paycheck Protection Program is healthy and interest free for your business if you use the funds provided towards the paying and retaining of your employees, and towards expenses (utilities, business lease payments, etc.) that fall within the guidelines dictated by the Small Business Administration. I mean it is 2.5 months of payroll. BOOM. Paid for. The EID loan has incredibly low interest rates so if you have some debt you need to pay off, this is an excellent chance to refinance that loan along with covering your overhead costs.

So, how do you know which one to apply for? Well I've got good news for you, my friends. You can apply for both of these programs separately![88] Though you may not be paid out on both of these programs simultaneously, I definitely recommend applying for both, immediately.

Now it's time to play the waiting game. We have done our part. We have filled out our portion, applications and supporting documents are submitted, now we wait to hear back from the government. An important thing to remember here is that NO ONE cares about your business, your livelihood, or your family like you do, or at all for that matter. Banker Joe is not making much money processing your loan application, so he is not going to have the same sense of urgency regarding this money as you will. His check will be the same no matter what speed he operates at. So what does this mean for you? You have got to follow up. Every. Single. Day. If you haven't heard back within a few days, it is up to you to make sure that they have everything they need. If not, you may go weeks waiting to hear from them only to learn that they need one more form. Time is money folks.

# 10 QUARANTINE JOKES THAT WILL HELP YOU FORGET THE FACT THAT YOU ARE STUCK AT HOME

With nothing to do at home, I am sure people are doing the horizontal mambo thus making a big baby boom happen. I would like to nominate in 2032 we start calling them quaranTEENS.

Do you want to hear a joke about the coronavirus? You probably won't get it.

You didn't stock up on toilet paper? You're sh*t outta luck now! They're all wiped out!

What's the difference between a Taco Bell meal and the coronavirus? You actually have a reason for your toilet paper hoarding with Taco Bell.

Day thirty without sports. Found a lady sitting on my couch yesterday. Apparently, she is my wife. She seems pretty cool.

Hopefully they make a movie about all of this directed by Quentin Quarantino.

They said that a mask and gloves were enough to go to the supermarket. They lied, everyone else had their clothes on, and I got asked to never come back.

Chuck Norris got exposed to the coronavirus. The virus is now under a "stay at home" order for a month.

The official social distancing rule: If you can smell their fart, move further apart.

What's the difference between the coronavirus and Bigfoot? You might catch Bigfoot.

**Don't think these are funny? Here is a bonus recipe for a "quarantini." After two of these, re-read the jokes and you will (probably) laugh.**

## QUARANTINI

*Serves one*

### INGREDIENTS

2 1/2 ounces gin or vodka

1/2 ounce dry vermouth

Ice

Lemon peel twist or olives, for garnish

### STEPS

*For shaken, NOT Stirred*

*(We aren't animals after all)*

1. Chill the glass: Before you build your quarantini, put your quarantini glass in the freezer to chill.
2. Build the drink: Place the gin or vodka and dry vermouth in a cocktail shaker.
3. Shake the drink: Add cubed ice and shake vigorously for ten seconds.
4. Strain the drink.
5. Garnish the drink: Pare a lemon peel, and express (pinch) the back of the lemon peel over the quarantini. Rub the lemon peel around the rim of the glass and drop it into the glass. Alternatively, garnish with speared olives.
6. ENJOY!

# ABOUT THE AUTHOR

Clay Clark is the host of an iTunes chart-topping podcast, the former United States Small Business Administration Entrepreneur, an author of fifteen books, the co-founder of five humans kids, and the founder of several multi-million dollar companies. Through this he has been featured on: Forbes, FastCompany, Bloomberg TV, Bloomberg Radio, Business Insider, Yahoo Finance, PandoDaily, Business Insider, Entrepreneurs On Fire, Fox, ABC, etc. Clay has been a contributing writer for Entrepreneur.com and Forbes.com. With a focus on both entertaining and educating, Yahoo Finance has described Clay Clark as "The Jim Carrey of entrepreneurship." Throughout his career, Clay has been the award-winning entertainer, educator, and speaker of choice for the world's top companies including: Hewlett Packard, Southwest Airlines, UPS, O'Reilly Auto Parts, Bama Companies, Boeing, Farmers Insurance, New York Life Insurance, Maytag University, Oral Roberts University, Oxi Fresh, QuikTrip, Valspar Paint, and countless other companies and organizations looking to engage, entertain, and educate their people.

# ENDNOTES

1     Akbari, Anna. "Why Your Smartphone Is Destroying Your Life." Psychology Today. Sussex Publishers, January 30, 2018. https://www.psychologytoday.com/us/blog/startup-your-life/201801/why-your-smartphone-is-destroying-your-life.

2     "Time Flies: U.S. Adults Now Spend Nearly Half a Day Interacting with Media." Nielsen. Accessed April 14, 2020. https://www.nielsen.com/us/en/insights/article/2018/time-flies-us-adults-now-spend-nearly-half-a-day-interacting-with-media/.

3     "The Burden of the Influenza A H1N1pdm09 Virus since the 2009 Pandemic." Centers for Disease Control and Prevention. Centers for Disease Control and Prevention, June 10, 2019. https://www.cdc.gov/flu/pandemic-resources/burden-of-h1n1.html.

4     See 1

5     https://www.youtube.com/watch?v=AO65alZzkog&feature=emb_logo

6     Bremner, Jade. "U.S. Alcohol Sales Increase 55 Percent in One Week Amid Coronavirus Pandemic." Newsweek. Newsweek, April 1, 2020. https://www.newsweek.com/us-alcohol-sales-increase-55-percent-one-week-amid-coronavirus-pandemic-1495510.

7    "Coronavirus Pandemic Boosts Marijuana Sales While Many Businesses Struggle." U.S. News & World Report. U.S. News & World Report. Accessed April 14, 2020. https://www.usnews.com/news/national-news/articles/2020-03-20/coronavirus-pandemic-boosts-marijuana-sales-while-many-businesses-struggle.

8    Freeman, James. "Opinion | Should We Wait Until Easter?" The Wall Street Journal. Dow Jones & Company, March 26, 2020. https://www.wsj.com/articles/should-we-wait-until-easter-11585239104.

9    Scutti, Susan. "Flu Season Deaths Top 80,000 Last Year, CDC Says." CNN. Cable News Network, September 27, 2018. https://www.cnn.com/2018/09/26/health/flu-deaths-2017--2018-cdc-bn/index.html.

10   Guzman, Joseph. "Are Kids Immune to Coronavirus? Scientists Say Children Show Surprising Resistance to COVID-19--but Could Still Be Spreading It." TheHill, April 4, 2020. https://thehill.com/changing-america/well-being/487504-children-arent-immune-to-coronavirus-but-theyve-largely-been.

11   Walker, Amara, and Melissa Alonso. "12-Year-Old Girl with Coronavirus Is on a Ventilator and Fighting for Her Life." CNN. Cable News Network, March 22, 2020. https://www.cnn.com/2020/03/22/us/georgia-coronavirus-girl-hospitalized/index.html.

12   Bloomberg.com. Bloomberg. Accessed April 14, 2020. https://www.bloomberg.com/news/articles/2020-03-

18/99-of-those-who-died-from-virus-had-other-illness-italy-says?__twitter_impression=true.

13    "FastStats - Leading Causes of Death." Centers for Disease Control and Prevention. Centers for Disease Control and Prevention, March 17, 2017. https://www.cdc.gov/nchs/fastats/leading-causes-of-death.htm.

14    Bernard, Tara Siegel, and Ron Lieber. "F.A.Q. on Stimulus Checks, Unemployment and the Coronavirus Plan." The New York Times. The New York Times, March 26, 2020. https://www.nytimes.com/article/coronavirus-stimulus-package-questions-answers.html.

15    "U.S. National Debt Clock : Real Time." U.S. National Debt Clock : Real Time. Accessed April 14, 2020. https://www.usdebtclock.org/.

16    "Chillingly, Scariest Coronavirus Death Toll May Not Come from COVID-19." CCN.com, March 19, 2020. https://www.ccn.com/chillingly-scariest-coronavirus-death-toll-may-not-come-from-covid-19/.

17    Belluz, Julia. "'We Are at a Turning Point': The Coronavirus Outbreak Is Looking More like a Pandemic." Vox. Vox, February 25, 2020. https://www.vox.com/2020/2/23/21149327/coronavirus-pandemic-meaning-italy.

18    Fink, Sheri. "Worst-Case Estimates for U.S. Coronavirus Deaths." The New York Times. The New York Times, March 13, 2020. https://www.nytimes.com/2020/03/13/us/coronavirus-deaths-estimate.html.

19    Rieder, Rem. "Trump and the Coronavirus Death
      Projections." FactCheck.org, March 30, 2020. https://
      www.factcheck.org/2020/03/trump-and-the-coronavi-
      rus-death-projections/.

20    "Remarks by President Trump, Vice President Pence,
      and Members of the Coronavirus Task Force in Press
      Briefing." The White House. The United States Gov-
      ernment. Accessed April 14, 2020. https://www.
      whitehouse.gov/briefings-statements/remarks-president-
      trump-vice-president-pence-members-coronavirus-task-
      force-press-briefing-3/.

21    Mervosh, Sarah, Denise Lu, and Vanessa Swales. "See
      Which States and Cities Have Told Residents to Stay at
      Home." The New York Times. The New York Times,
      March 24, 2020. https://www.nytimes.com/interac-
      tive/2020/us/coronavirus-stay-at-home-order.html.

22    Rieder, Rem. "Trump and the Coronavirus Death
      Projections." FactCheck.org, March 30, 2020. https://
      www.factcheck.org/2020/03/trump-and-the-coronavi-
      rus-death-projections/.

23    Fauci, Anthony S., Q. Li, J. Grein, Y. Zhang, N.
      van Doremalen, and National Institute of Allergy.
      "Covid-19 - Navigating the Uncharted: NEJM." New
      England Journal of Medicine, March 26, 2020. https://
      www.nejm.org/doi/full/10.1056/NEJMe2002387.

24    Baker, Peter, and Maggie Haberman. "Behind Trump's
      Reversal on Reopening the Country: 2 Sets of Num-

bers." The New York Times. The New York Times, March 31, 2020. https://www.nytimes.com/2020/03/30/ us/politics/trump-coronavirus.html?action=click&module=RelatedLinks&pgtype=Article.

25    Marsh, Julia, and Vincent Barone. "Coronavirus Killing People in New York City at Rate of One Every 17 Minutes." New York Post. New York Post, March 28, 2020. https://nypost.com/2020/03/27/another-84-people-killed-by-coronavirus-in-new-york-city/.

26    TodayShow. "Number of US Coronavirus Deaths Now Exceeds 9/11 Death Toll." TODAY.com. Accessed April 14, 2020. https://www.today.com/video/number-of-us-coronavirus-deaths-now-exceeds-9-11-death-toll-81421893740.

27    O'Reilly, Andrew. "White House Projects 100K to 240K Coronavirus Deaths as Trump Tells US to Prepare for 'Very Painful Two Weeks'." Fox News. FOX News Network, March 31, 2020. https://www.foxnews.com/ politics/trump-tells-americans-to-prepare-for-a-very-painful-two-weeks-as-white-house-releases-extended-coronavirus-guidelines.

28    "Personal Protective Equipment: Questions and Answers." Centers for Disease Control and Prevention. Centers for Disease Control and Prevention, March 14, 2020. https://www.cdc.gov/coronavirus/2019-ncov/hcp/ respirator-use-faq.html.

29    "Archived Estimated Influenza Illnesses, Medical

Visits, Hospitalizations, and Deaths in the United States - 2017–2018 Influenza Season." Centers for Disease Control and Prevention. Centers for Disease Control and Prevention, November 22, 2019. https://www.cdc.gov/flu/about/burden/2017-2018/archive.htm.

30    "Older Adults." Centers for Disease Control and Prevention. Centers for Disease Control and Prevention, April 7, 2020. https://www.cdc.gov/coronavirus/2019-ncov/need-extra-precautions/older-adults.html.

31    Bloomberg.com. Bloomberg. Accessed April 14, 2020. https://www.bloomberg.com/news/articles/2020-03-18/99-of-those-who-died-from-virus-had-other-illness-italy-says?__twitter_impression=true.

32    Chavez, Nicole, and Amanda Watts. "Here's What We Know about the 100 People Who've Died in the US from Coronavirus." CNN. Cable News Network, March 18, 2020. https://www.cnn.com/2020/03/17/health/coronavirus-united-states-deaths/index.html.

33    "Age, Sex, Existing Conditions of COVID-19 Cases and Deaths." Worldometer. Accessed April 14, 2020. https://www.worldometers.info/coronavirus/coronavirus-age-sex-demographics/.

34    Walker, Amara, and Melissa Alonso. "12-Year-Old Girl with Coronavirus Is on a Ventilator and Fighting for Her Life." CNN. Cable News Network, March 22, 2020. https://www.cnn.com/2020/03/22/us/geor-

gia-coronavirus-girl-hospitalized/index.html.

35    William Wan, Joel Achenbach. "Coronavirus Is
      Mysteriously Sparing Kids and Killing the Elderly.
      Understanding Why May Help Defeat the Virus." The
      Washington Post. WP Company, March 10, 2020.
      https://www.washingtonpost.com/health/2020/03/10/
      coronavirus-is-mysteriously-sparing-kids-killing-elder-
      ly-understanding-why-may-help-defeat-virus/.

36    Bendix, Aria. "Only a Handful of Children Have Been
      Diagnosed with the Coronavirus - and Experts Have a
      Few Guesses as to Why." Business Insider. Business
      Insider, March 13, 2020. https://www.businessinsider.
      com/coronavirus-case-children-infants-low-disease-ex-
      pert-explain-why-2020-2.

37    Smith, Stephen. "Coronavirus Has Spared American
      Children. The Flu Has Killed 144 Kids so Far This
      Season." CBS News. CBS Interactive, March 16, 2020.
      https://www.cbsnews.com/news/coronavirus-has-large-
      ly-spared-us-children-the-flu-has-killed-144-so-far-this-
      season/.

38    Smith, Stephen. "Coronavirus Has Spared American
      Children. The Flu Has Killed 144 Kids so Far This
      Season." CBS News. CBS Interactive, March 16, 2020.
      https://www.cbsnews.com/news/coronavirus-has-large-
      ly-spared-us-children-the-flu-has-killed-144-so-far-this-
      season/.

39    Creitz, Charles. "Minnesota Doctor Blasts 'Ridicu-

lous' CDC Coronavirus Death Count Guidelines." Fox
News. FOX News Network, April 9, 2020. https://www.
foxnews.com/media/physician-blasts-cdc-coronavi-
rus-death-count-guidelines.

40    See note 44

41    *Dr. Deborah Birx |Recording Covid-19 as Cause of Death
No Matter What. YouTube.com*, 2020, www.youtube.
com/watch?v=GGHp1GdOD4k&feature=emb_logo .


42    Ray Sipherd, special to CNBC.com. "The Third-Lead-
ing Cause of Death in US Most Doctors Don't Want
You to Know About." CNBC. CNBC, February 28,
2018. https://www.cnbc.com/2018/02/22/medical-er-
rors-third-leading-cause-of-death-in-america.html.

43    Bloomberg.com. Bloomberg. Accessed April 14, 2020.
https://www.bloomberg.com/news/articles/2019-02-13/
traffic-deaths-in-u-s-exceed-40-000-for-third-straight-
year.

44    "Heart Disease Facts." Centers for Disease Control and
Prevention. Centers for Disease Control and Prevention,
December 2, 2019. https://www.cdc.gov/heartdisease/
facts.htm.

45    Center for Drug Evaluation and Research. "Frequently Asked Questions about the FDA Drug Approval
Process." U.S. Food and Drug Administration. FDA.
Accessed April 14, 2020. https://www.fda.gov/drugs/
special-features/frequently-asked-questions-about-fda-

drug-approval-process#3.

46    Commissioner, Office of the. "Fast Track." U.S. Food
and Drug Administration. FDA. Accessed April 14,
2020. https://www.fda.gov/patients/fast-track-break-
through-therapy-accelerated-approval-priority-review/
fast-track.

47    "Drugs@FDA: FDA-Approved Drugs." accessdata.
fda.gov. Accessed April 14, 2020. https://www.access-
data.fda.gov/scripts/cder/daf/index.cfm?event=over-
view.process&varApplNo=009768.

48
"Tulsa To Begin Shelter In Place Order Sunday." News On 6.
Accessed April 14, 2020. https://www.newson6.com/
story/41949474/tulsa-to-begin-shelter-in-place-order-
sunday.

49    "COVID-19 Online Sales Impact Data." Quantum
Metric, March 20, 2020. https://www.quantummetric.
com/covid-19-online-sales-impact/.

50    "Amazon Remains the Undisputed No. 1." eMarketer.
Accessed April 14, 2020. https://www.emarketer.com/
content/amazon-remains-the-undisputed-no-1.

51    Clark, Dave. "Amazon Ramps Hiring, Opening
100,000 New Roles to Support People Relying on
Amazon's Service in This Stressful Time." US Day One
Blog. Amazon, April 14, 2020. https://blog.aboutam-
azon.com/operations/amazon-opening-100000-new-
roles.

52    Etherington, Darrell. "Amazon Limiting Shipments of Certain Types of Products Due to COVID-19 Pandemic." TechCrunch. TechCrunch, March 17, 2020. https://techcrunch.com/2020/03/17/amazon-limiting-shipments-to-certain-types-of-products-due-to-covid-19-pandemic/.

53    Isidore, Chris. "More than Half of American Jobs Are at Risk Because of Coronavirus." CNN. Cable News Network, March 17, 2020. https://www.cnn.com/2020/03/16/economy/job-losses-coronavirus/index.html.

54    "Government Is Not Reason: Constitution Preservation." Government is not reason | Constitution Preservation. Accessed April 14, 2020. https://www.constitutionpreservation.org/articles/april-2-2014/government-not-reason.

55    Allyn, Bobby. "Fauci Estimates That 100,000 To 200,000 Americans Could Die From The Coronavirus." NPR. NPR, March 29, 2020. https://www.npr.org/sections/coronavirus-live-updates/2020/03/29/823517467/fauci-estimates-that-100-000-to-200-000-americans-could-die-from-the-coronavirus.

56    DeSilver, Drew. "10 Facts about American Workers." Pew Research Center. Pew Research Center, August 29, 2019. https://www.pewresearch.org/fact-tank/2019/08/29/facts-about-american-workers/.

57    Carmody, Bill. "Why 96 Percent of Businesses Fail Within 10 Years." Inc.com. Inc., August 12, 2015. https://www.inc.com/bill-carmody/why-96-of-business-es-fail-within-10-years.html.58      "US Business Firmographics – Company Size." NAICS Association. Accessed April 14, 2020. https://www.naics.com/business-lists/counts-by-company-size/.

59    Statista. "Topic: Physicians." www.statista.com. Accessed April 14, 2020. https://www.statista.com/topics/1244/physicians/.

60    Shea, Molly. "Cancer Deaths Went up during the Recession." New York Post. New York Post, May 26, 2016. https://nypost.com/2016/05/26/cancer-deaths-went-up-during-the-recession/.

61    "OECD." Wikipedia. Wikimedia Foundation, March 25, 2020. https://en.wikipedia.org/wiki/OECD.

62    Nichols, Hannah. "The Top 10 Leading Causes of Death in the United States." Medical News Today. MediLexicon International, July 4, 2019. https://www.medicalnewstoday.com/articles/282929#cancer.

63    Krauskopf, Lewis. "'D' Word Rears Head as Coronavirus-Hit Markets Brace for Recession." Reuters. Thomson Reuters, March 17, 2020. https://www.reuters.com/article/uk-health-coronavirus-stocks-economy-usa/d-word-rears-head-as-coronavirus-hit-markets-brace-for-recession-idUSKBN2140IA.

64    "American Revolution Facts." American Battlefield

Trust, April 6, 2020. https://www.battlefields.org/learn/articles/american-revolution-faqs.

65    "White House Projects Grim Toll From Coronavirus." The New York Times. The New York Times. Accessed April 14, 2020. https://www.nytimes.com/2020/03/31/world/coronavirus-news.html.

66    Rick Noack, Meryl Kornfield. "White House Task Force Projects 100,000 to 240,000 Deaths in U.S., Even with Mitigation Efforts." The Washington Post. WP Company, April 1, 2020. https://www.washingtonpost.com/world/2020/03/31/coronavirus-latest-news/.

67    Garza, Alejandro de la. "How Social Media Is Shaping Our Fears of the Coronavirus." Time. Time, March 16, 2020. https://time.com/5802802/social-media-coronavirus/.

68    "Psychology: Why Bad News Dominates the Headlines." BBC Future. BBC, July 29, 2014. https://www.bbc.com/future/article/20140728-why-is-all-the-news-bad.

69    "Negativity Bias." Wikipedia. Wikimedia Foundation, March 11, 2020. https://en.wikipedia.org/wiki/Negativity_bias.

70    Caprino, Kathy. "The Top 5 Reasons People Don't Make The Changes They Long For." Forbes. Forbes Magazine, May 29, 2017. https://www.forbes.com/sites/kathycaprino/2017/05/26/the-top-5-reasons-people-

dont-make-the-changes-they-long-for/#78f8ce714674.

71  "White House Projects Grim Toll From Coronavirus." The New York Times. The New York Times, March 31, 2020. https://www.nytimes.com/2020/03/31/world/coronavirus-live-news-updates.html.

72  "FastStats - Leading Causes of Death." Centers for Disease Control and Prevention. Centers for Disease Control and Prevention, March 17, 2017. https://www.cdc.gov/nchs/fastats/leading-causes-of-death.htm.

73  Friedman, Ron. "Is Your Smartphone Making You Dumb?" Psychology Today. Sussex Publishers, January 6, 2015. https://www.psychologytoday.com/us/blog/glue/201501/is-your-smartphone-making-you-dumb.

74  Walton, Alice G. "6 Ways Social Media Affects Our Mental Health." Forbes. Forbes Magazine, October 3, 2017. https://www.forbes.com/sites/alicegwalton/2017/06/30/a-run-down-of-social-medias-effects-on-our-mental-health/#70d7d9812e5a.

75  Kross, Ethan, Philippe Verduyn, Emre Demiralp, David Seungjae Lee, Natalie Lin, Holly Shablack, John Jonides, and Oscar Ybarra. "Facebook Use Predicts Declines in Subjective Well-Being in Young Adults." PLOS ONE. Public Library of Science. Accessed April 14, 2020. https://journals.plos.org/plosone/article?id=10.1371/journal.pone.0069841&mbid=synd_msnhealth#s2.

76  Sun, Carolyn. "How Do Your Social Media Habits

Compare to the Average Person's?" Entrepreneur, December 14, 2017. https://www.entrepreneur.com/slideshow/306136.

77  Hadad, Chuck. "#Being13: Teens and Social Media." CNN. Cable News Network, October 13, 2015. https://www.cnn.com/2015/10/05/health/being-13-teens-social-media-study/index.html.

78  Wallace, Kelly. "Teens Spend 9 Hours a Day Using Media, Report Says." CNN. Cable News Network, November 4, 2015. https://www.cnn.com/2015/11/03/health/teens-tweens-media-screen-use-report/.

79  "Mark Manson: The Best-Selling Author of The Subtle Art of Not Giving a F$%k." The ThriveTime Show, February 18, 2020. https://www.thrivetimeshow.com/business-podcasts/mark-manson-the-best-selling-author-of-the-subtle-art-of-not-giving-a-fk/.

80  ABC News. ABC News Network. Accessed April 14, 2020. https://abcnews.go.com/Politics/calls-us-helpline-jump-891-white-house-warned/story?id=70010113.

81  Valinsky, Jordan. "Booze Sales Are Booming as People Stockpile Alcohol ... but It May Not Last." CNN. Cable News Network, April 1, 2020. https://www.cnn.com/2020/04/01/business/alcohol-sales-coronavirus-trnd/index.html.

82  Bloomberg.com. Bloomberg. Accessed April 14, 2020. https://www.bloomberg.com/news/articles/2020-03-18/99-of-those-who-died-from-virus-had-other-illness-

italy-says?__twitter_impression=true.

83    Leonard, Kimberly. "Doctors and Nurses Are Get-
      ting Hit with Pay Cuts, Layoffs, and Furloughs Even
      as They Fight the Coronavirus Pandemic." Business
      Insider. Business Insider, April 2, 2020. https://www.
      businessinsider.com/economic-turmoil-from-coronavi-
      rus-pandemic-hits-doctors-nurses-2020-3.

84    Jones, Corey. "Double-Whammy: Hospitals Face
      Dilemma of Furloughs amid COVID-19 Needed Care."
      Tulsa World, April 7, 2020. https://www.tulsaworld.
      com/news/local/double-whammy-hospitals-face-di-
      lemma-of-furloughs-amid-covid-19-needed-care/arti-
      cle_e2e0df4f-2449-5598-a7e4-be18e80d89c5.html.

85    "A Visualization of the CARES Act." Committee for
      a Responsible Federal Budget, March 30, 2020. http://
      www.crfb.org/blogs/visualization-cares-act.

86    Small Business Administration. Accessed April 14,
      2020. https://www.sba.gov/local-assistance/find/?-
      type=SBA District Office&pageNumber=1.

87    "Disaster Loan Assistance." SBA. Accessed April 14,
      2020. https://covid19relief.sba.gov/#/.

88    Committee on Small Business. "Cares Flow Chart."
      2020. PDF file.
https://smallbusiness.house.gov/uploadedfiles/cares_flow_
      chart_edit.pdf